En

Curtis Wallace, a trusted source for leadership and strategy, enriches the pursuit of transformational change in his book, *Elevating Excellence*. This provocative work encourages us all to exude excellence without excuse and to experience the exhilaration of exponential outcomes.

BISHOP EDGAR L. VANN
Second Ebenezer, Detroit, Michigan

If you read only one memoir concerning excellence, make it this one. Wallace resurrects the narrative of a lost art.

PASTOR KEION HENDERSON
Lighthouse Church, Houston, Texas

Nothing is worse than failing while trying but not knowing why. In this book, Curtis Wallace answers that question for ministry leaders. Thanks for filling the gap!

BISHOP JAMES DIXON
Community of Faith Church, Houston, Texas

Curtis Wallace is emerging as one of today's anchor voices on leadership. He gets it! In *Elevating Excellence* he provides a clear road map to stay current and relevant in our fast-paced world.

TIM CLINTON, ED.D., LPC, LMFT
President, American Association of Christian Counselors

No matter what business you're in or what kind of leader you are, Curtis' book will help you make an impact, make a difference and make the most of the blessings you've been given. If you're looking for a way to 'inspire for higher,' *Elevating Excellence* is it! Whether it's running my production company or my charity, Curtis' insights and examples of leadership have given me lots of tools to put to use right away.

LEEZA GIBBONS
TV & Radio Show Host
New York Times Bestselling author of *Take2*

ELEVATING EXCELLENCE

ELEVATING EXCELLENCE

10

Defining Choices that Lead to Relevance

CURTIS WALLACE

DESTINY IMAGE® PUBLISHERS, INC.

P.O. Box 310, Shippensburg, PA 17257-0310

"Promoting Inspired Lives."

This book and all other Destiny Image, Revival Press, MercyPlace, Fresh Bread, Destiny Image Fiction, and Treasure House books are available at Christian bookstores and distributors worldwide.

For a U.S. bookstore nearest you, call 1-800-722-6774.

For more information on foreign distributors, call 717-532-3040.

Reach us on the Internet: www.destinyimage.com.

ISBN 13 TP: 978-0-7684-0343-5

ISBN 13 Ebook: 978-0-7684-8494-6

For Worldwide Distribution, Printed in the U.S.A.

1 2 3 4 5 6 7 8 / 17 16 15 14 13

Acknowledgments

One of the things I like to say about Bishop T. D. Jakes is that as good as you think he is on the stage in front of 50,000 people, he is exponentially better one-on-one. I have had the unique opportunity to have more than my share of that one-on-one time over the last 12 years of working with him. In those times he has poured so much into my life. I want to acknowledge him here and thank him for that.

I also want to thank my dad and mom, Jimmy and Joyce Wallace, for all of their sacrifices, and for making sure I always knew I was loved and that I could achieve anything I wanted. They also taught me the value of work. Growing up, I saw my dad get up early and go to work six days a week. That example had an impact on my life and my own work habits. Moreover, they continue to do the same for my children and I am grateful for that. I may be an executive, movie producer, and an author, but a librarian and a barber are the ones who have lived true lives of relevance.

Contents

PREFACE

I've had the absolute privilege of spending the last 12 years of my professional life working with Bishop T. D. Jakes at TDJ Enterprises. I've worked on projects ranging from gospel stage plays like *Woman Thou Art Loosed* and *Behind Closed Doors* to movies like *Jumping the Broom* and *Sparkle*, as well as various music projects, books, and conferences. It has truly been an incredible ride.

One of the great personal benefits of my time with Bishop Jakes has been the tremendous diversity and quality of people I have worked with and developed relationships with over the years. Having worked with such a diverse array of talented and successful people from varied worlds and perspectives has given me the unique opportunity to see, close up, what success and relevance really mean.

Executives are different from musicians, who are also different from actors. They each have their own unique perspective on what it takes to create meaningful success in today's world. When I combine the influence of all of these talented and driven people with the best opportunity of all—the chance to spend extended amounts of one-on-one time with Bishop Jakes—it has given me a perspective that I believe few people will ever have.

I'm currently moving into the next phase of my professional life, making the transition from COO of TDJ Enterprises to president of Ascension Advisory Group where I will be focused on what we call "elevating excellence." To me, elevating excellence simply involves working with great people and organizations, helping them achieve higher levels of success in their business, ministry, and life.

As you read this book, you will notice that it is really about two simple yet often elusive concepts: relevance and choices. Based on my experience, relevance is what the search is for. At the end of the day, more than money or power or anything else we may attain in life, we all want to know that our life and our work mattered—that is was relevant. In turn, I believe that it is the choices we make every day, both the big and small ones, that determine whether we lead lives of relevance or not.

I will be discussing throughout this book ten characteristics I believe are shared by great leaders—people who have achieved relevance in a world seemingly too full of meaningless, insignificant fluff. In a world where you can now be famous for just being famous, these are the ten characteristics that separate the relevant from insignificance.

You're probably wondering now where the choices come into play, for it is about relevance *and* choices. Very simply, it is the choices we make every day that determines whether we are exemplifying these ten characteristics or not. Life is cumulative. Every spending decision we make, no matter how small, will over the course of a lifetime add up to our fortune or lack thereof. Some decisions to spend add to the fortune (our investments) and some spending decisions (those fun but sometimes unnecessary purchases, such as frivolous shopping sprees) take away from it. The same logic applies to incorporating these ten characteristics into your personal and professional life.

While this book is written to and for everyone—because I believe that we all are leaders in some capacity—you will notice that in most chapters I have included a "Special Note for the Church." These notes are included because I believe that part of my calling is to help churches and other charities develop extraordinary leaders. The reason is simple: our churches and non-profits have an incredibly difficult mission to accomplish. It will take special leaders to help them declare "Mission Accomplished." While these sections are labeled as being for the church, I hope that everyone reading this book will read these sections and take them to heart. The situation or circumstance may be church specific, but the principles are universal.

I hope you enjoy the journey.

THE SEARCH FOR RELEVANCE

Throughout this book I'm going to discuss in detail ten specific characteristics I believe today's leaders need to understand and incorporate into their decision-making process. If we embrace these concepts, they will naturally start to become reflected in the cumulative effect of the multitude of decisions we all make each and every day.

However, for the ideas in this book to be most effective, you need to understand and embrace those points that make you and your organization relevant. What I mean by this is that, in practical terms, there are points of differentiation. What is your competitive edge? What is it that you do that others do not? What do you do well within your organization?

Every person, every company, and every ministry has its unique points of relevance. For example, an established company may have the advantage of a great well-known brand. At the same time, a small rival start-up without the brand name will need to find and exploit its competitive edge if it is to be successful in the world. There has to be something that sets it apart from all other companies.

One of the great things about God is that he made each of us different. That means no one else has your unique combination of life experience, education, work experience, and worldview—not to mention all of the intangibles like drive, determination, work ethic, and attitude. This means, very simply, that no matter what your current station in life, no matter what you have or have not accomplished in life, there is *no one* who can offer the world what you can offer. This is because you are the only *you*, and no one else can bring the tools and perspectives you can bring to any particular situation. Once you put together your point of relevance with decision-making based on that point of relevance, success will surely follow.

Special Note for the Church

While this book is intended for leaders from all areas of life, I will from time to time have special notes for those in ministry. The church today has unique challenges in the search for relevance. The modern church faces competition on a myriad of fronts. We live in an on-demand world where everything from movies to books to hundreds of television channels to video games to ever-expanding social media is available to us at the push of a button. That adds up to unprecedented competition for the hearts and minds of the population. Never before has the church encountered this level of competition.

Not only does the church face the external competition described, but there is also a highly competitive landscape within. In the age of the megachurch and the multilocation church, there is immense competition within the larger body of Christ. Just as we no longer have to watch television by appointment, we also no longer have to attend church by appointment. In fact, on Sunday mornings in America, you can now virtually participate with some of the best churches in the country, no matter where you live. People don't even have to get out of bed and they can watch the entire Potter's House church service being streamed live on the Internet. You can do the same thing with Joel Osteen or 100 other pastors around the country. This raises a question to me of how the local church maintains its relevance in the face of competition like it has never faced before, both from within and without the church. Why is it that I want to choose to get up on Sunday morning and take my family to *your* church? What is it that is special about that experience that makes me want to be a part of your church?

Not only is it facing both internal and external competition, but over the last few years heightened economic challenges are facing the church as well. The economic downturn that we've encountered since 2008 has hurt the business world in general. However, the church world has probably been hit harder than any other segment of the economy, just because of the reality that donations are the first to go when a family faces economic distress.

This happens because donations are not contractual in nature—they're not a mortgage payment, they're not rent, they're not a car payment. As a result of this our churches have been stressed financially in a way that they have never been stressed before. Then, at the same time that churches are under stress, the banks are pulling away from the churches—five and ten years ago, the banks were anxious to do business with the churches; but now they're pulling back. All of these factors together are creating an incredibly challenging environment for the church today.

And in order to meet that challenge we're going to have to have a new level of leadership. There are going to have to be leaders in the church who are ready and prepared to meet those challenges. But the good news is that it is also a time of great opportunity within the church. Because of those same things that we just talked about in terms of creating competition for the church, the church has the ability to use those same tools to be successful in these trying times.

A great example of finding relevance in the world of ministry actually comes from outside the church world. A good friend of mine, Dr. Aaron Tabor, who is a medical doctor and a pastor's kid, started a Facebook page four years ago called Jesus Daily. Today, you could argue that Dr. Tabor runs one of the most effective ministries in the world. How can that be possible? How can a single individual, with no real budget, no name, and a laptop go from zero to one of the world's largest ministries (at least in terms of the number of people he impacts on a daily basis)? It's simple: he found a point of relevance.

Before most ministries even had a Facebook page, he embraced the technology wholeheartedly. He gave the Facebook generation their little dose of Jesus—starting by doing things as simple as putting Scriptures and quotes and pictures on Jesus Daily several times a day. Over time, he learned the "science" and the "art" of Facebook; and with a laser focus, Dr. Tabor kept refining and improving Jesus Daily.

Not only does Jesus Daily have a huge audience in terms of sheer numbers it reaches on a daily basis, but it also consistently has the highest level of engagement of any page on Facebook. It is one thing to have a lot of followers on Facebook (or people who have "liked" your Facebook page), but the real measure of effectiveness is whether or not the audience is truly engaged. When you post something, do people react? Do they "comment" on or "like" the post? By this measure, Jesus Daily is among the top Facebook pages—it's not some celebrity page, but a page about Jesus that is run by a medical doctor.

Think about the level of influence Dr. Tabor and Jesus Daily have achieved. This guy, without a large ministry and with no real budget to speak of, can now reach and influence millions of people through the Internet. He can pull out his phone, type a sentence, press send, and make the lives of millions of people better with a little bit of inspiration as they go through their day. Dr. Tabor found his point of relevance, focused on it, built a brand, created an experience for his audience, and the result is a ministry of tremendous influence.

Just think about how, when properly applied, the Dr. Tabor example can positively influence your business or ministry. I was recently in Houston, Texas, speaking to the leadership of my good friend, Bishop James Dixon's church, Community of Faith. I was addressing about 200 core leaders—the diehard supporters—who were looking for ways to grow the church. I gave them a simple, cost-free challenge: if everyone of those 200 core supporters would take 30 seconds a day to post a message about something that was said or happened at church, then 4,000 people a day would be getting positive messages about Community of Faith through the Internet. (This is based on if the 200 people post a message that is then seen by another 200 people [the average number of Facebook friends most people have], then 4,000 people will see it in a short period of time [200 x 200 = 4,000]. Think about the power of that!)

It sounds easy to do (and at the individual level it is), but it takes many of the leadership characteristics in this book to pull it off. It takes focus, on both the part of the leaders and the followers, to send messages on a consistent basis. It takes teamwork to get the messages to the people. It takes coaching so that everyone can learn the best practices for effective Facebook messaging. It also takes an understanding of the power of the church's brand so that the messages reinforce the brand. And it also means the leadership must understand what they don't know and get help to fill in the gaps of their knowledge and experience.

At the end of the day, while we have tremendous challenges and stress in the church, we also have incredible opportunity for those who are willing to look at things a little bit differently, for those who are willing to be leaders, taking some chances, getting out there and getting things done. We have an incredible time of opportunity before us, because, as everybody knows, out of all this chaos there is something special that is going to arise. We have potential because when we think about the challenge and the competition, just remember this: the church is selling the best product in the world. Not only that, but we're giving it away for free. If you can't sell the best product in the world for free, then something is terribly wrong.

So let's continue while I share what I think some of the characteristics leaders today need to value and hold dear as they guide their organizations. This, to me, is really the biggest part of what a leader does. By definition, a leader is that person at the top of an organization who holds the core values, and who transfers those values to the staff and to the rest of the organization. Because of this, there are certain values that, if the leader possesses and holds those things to be important, will flow through the organization and help lead it to success.

KNOW YOURSELF

Chapter 1

THE BIG IDEA

How many times have you heard someone say, "I wish I had thought of that"? It is a constant refrain that most of us hear on a continual basis. People are always lamenting that they were not responsible for some great idea that led to a successful enterprise. If only they had been the one to have that idea, they too could be enjoying the fruits of success. When I hear these kinds of comments repeatedly, my thought is always the same: *Well, yes and no.*

Real leaders recognize that there are two issues present here. The first is that I absolutely know that a single big idea can be the starting point on the road to success. In fact, it is almost always a single thought or idea that propels an individual to go down a path that leads to the creation of a great organization or product. However, I also believe that most people get great ideas all the time.

What then is the distinguishing factor that keeps those from having the idea from those who implement it and benefit from it? It is simply this: the people who understand the power of a single big idea, believe in their idea so much and pursue it with a relentless tenacity that makes everyone else stand around and say, "I wish I had thought of that." The sad reality is that if most people had the idea, the world would never know about it. Why? Because even though there is tremendous power in the idea, the idea has no meaning alone—it has to be implemented.

Just as faith without works is empty, the idea without the belief in it and a willingness to turn it into reality is nothing but a thought—just some mist in the midst of a storm.

The Power of the Idea

There are countless examples of people who have taken the "big idea" and gone on to turn that single God-given moment of inspiration into a lifetime of meaningful success and contribution. I just found out that this year marks the 20th anniversary of the publication of Bishop Jakes's first book, *Woman, Thou Art Loosed!* This self-published book, which has gone on to sell more than 5 million copies, is a great example of the power of the big idea.

Back in the early 1990s, Bishop Jakes realized that he was hearing the same themes over and over again from the women he was counseling. He realized that there was an unmet need among women who had been victims of abuse. As a pastor, he also realized that the Bible had answers for these women (this was the big idea—that he could use Scripture to help hurting women to heal and move on). Then, in an effort to address the need, he taught a Sunday school class. He didn't get finished the first Sunday, so it carried over into the second one. And the attendance for that class on the second Sunday was double of the previous class. At this point he realized that he was hitting on something and so he continued to pursue it.

He took a leap of faith in his big idea. Taking money from his savings account, he self-published his book, *Woman, Thou Art Loosed!* He typed it in the notepad on his computer because he didn't know how to use a word processor. This small-time preacher in West Virginia typed this book out himself on his notepad, then he took his savings and had some copies of the book printed, and went out and sold copies of the book wherever he went to preach. Eventually, a publisher picked the book up and it sold millions of copies.

Later, the book inspired the *Woman, Thou Art Loosed!* Conference, and then it inspired the *Woman, Thou Art Loosed!* stage play that Tyler Perry wrote and directed. Later still it became the award-winning *Woman, Thou Art Loosed!* movie. And this year it became a new *Woman, Thou Art Loosed* movie called *On the Seventh Day,* starring Blair Underwood. As you can see, that single idea that Bishop Jakes was given and that he had the faith to follow through on has spawned one of the great present-day ministries.

Think for a moment about the takeaways from this brief story. First, it doesn't matter where you are right now. Bishop Jakes was a preacher at a relatively small church in West Virginia. He didn't have any publishing connections; he didn't have a television ministry at that point; he didn't even know how to use word processing software on his computer. But the point is that it doesn't matter what your circumstances are right now; when God is ready, he can give you that one idea that can change the course of your future. The issue is going to be what you're going to do with it when it comes. Bishop Jakes was ready for his idea, and he believed in it, was persistent with it, kept going at it, and kept pushing on it until he built an organization out of it.

J. K. Rowling, the author of the *Harry Potter* books, was a single mother with no job and little in the way of prospects. However, she had an idea for a children's book and the dedication and passion to see it through. She took her one idea and turned it into the best-selling book series of all time. And along the way, she became one of the world's wealthiest women. And all of it came from one idea that captured her attention.

Remember that regardless of what your current circumstances are, God can give you the breath of an idea at any moment he so chooses. It is then your responsibility to pursue that idea. That is the genius of God's plan for us. He made each of us unique. Nobody else is going to have that particular idea or the ability to do something with that idea. Because you are unique, no one else will have your perspective on the problem or issue, or the inspiration to address the idea you've been given.

THE POINT OF RELEVANCE

As we get ready to move on, let's look a little deeper at this simple yet powerful concept. Don't think only the few brilliant minds are the ones who get the "big idea" that can be the basis of meaningful success. History has proven over and over again how unlikely people can achieve extraordinary relevance. Also, it is important to remember that your big idea may not be a new idea at all. It could just be a new and different way of presenting something that has been around for a long time.

George Lucas, the creator of such film franchises as *Star Wars* and *Indiana Jones*, recently sold his company, LucasFilm, to Disney for a price over $4 billion. Lucas built his career and fortune on the *Star Wars* franchise. When you think about it, the original film was both groundbreaking and not. From a story standpoint, *Star Wars* is as old as time—the story is built on ancient archetypes of good versus evil, love and family, and, yes, even unlikely heroes. But what is unique is that George Lucas was able to harness new technology to present an age-old story in a new and fresh way.

So no matter what your business endeavor in life may bring, it needs to be built on your big idea. It is the big idea that becomes your point of relevance—that is why someone chooses to do business with you and not your competitor.

To truly separate yourself or your business, there needs to be that one thing that sets you apart from all others, that makes you distinct and competitive.

In business, the last thing you want is to have your product or service become a commodity that is exactly the same as the product or service sold by your competitors. Why? Because when there is no point of distinction among competing products, competition becomes all about the price. This happened to PC makers. While makers like Dell, HP, and others were killing each other in price competition (because the machines they sold were largely similar), Apple was able to stay out of the price race because they actually sold a different product.

In some cases, price itself can be the big idea. One of my favorite companies is Southwest Airlines. While other airlines were losing vast amounts of money, Southwest was consistently profitable. And one reason is that Southwest was built on a big idea to be the "low cost" airline. Because the airline was built on that idea and its decision-making process reflected its low cost approach, Southwest was best positioned to succeed in a world where, to a large degree, air travel has become a commodity. At the same time, other airlines built on the idea of being the biggest or something amorphous like "the best" were not as well equipped to compete.

This is why it's important to capture your big idea and let it influence all of your decisions and life. For without a big idea that guides your life or organization, you will have no ability to focus.

Chapter 2

THE ABILITY TO FOCUS

The next characteristic of uncommon leaders I want to address is the ability to focus. I address this first because I believe that focus, or the ability of focus in a world full of distractions and competing options to keep the main thing the main thing, combined with a clear understanding of your point of relevance is a big step to seeing success on your path.

Since today's world is full of so many distractions, options, and even opportunities, you must have a filter through which ideas must pass. Let me give you an example from the world of movie making. Ever since Bishop T. D. Jakes and I started working in film and having some level of success, we have been inundated with scripts and proposals for movie projects. Very quickly we had to learn that we have to sort through hundreds of options to find the one film we want to make.

In order to sift through all of the options and find the right projects, we had to apply the concepts of relevance and focus. At TDJ Enterprises, our mantra was to produce products (whether a film, a book, or a music project) that educate, empower, and entertain. In other words, we wanted to be involved in projects that can make people's lives better—that is what Bishop Jakes's ministry is all about. We also know that we are most effective when we are involved in projects where Bishop Jakes's understanding of his audience and our ability to reach that audience can make a difference. Finally, the project has to line up with the brand of Bishop Jakes and his ministry because we do not want to do a film project, even if it will be successful, if it is going to negatively impact other things we do.

The result is that we have made good choices. Our projects have been successful and we have avoided both creative and business failures while consistently reinforcing the value of our brand and status in both Hollywood and in the ministry world.

Meaningful Focus

When considering the power of focus, there are two areas where it is meaningful. On a macro level, the ability to focus relates to the ability to keep yourself, your business, or your ministry focused on your point of relevance. Whatever it is that sets you apart, that is where you focus your efforts. There are some great examples of this type of focus in the business world.

I read a lot of biographies (I personally believe that people who want to achieve a fulfilling, successful, and relevant life need to be exposed to others who have done so, and biographies can be good way to get that exposure). One of my recent favorites is *Steve Jobs* by Walter Isaacson. Steve Jobs, who died in October of 2011, was one of the founders of Apple Computers. At one point he left Apple and then later returned to become CEO when the company was in trouble.

When Jobs returned to the company that he had co-founded, he took what seemed to be drastic action. He cut the Apple product line from 350 products to 10. The reason for the drastic cut in the product line was simple: Steve Jobs understood the power of focus. He wanted every product that Apple made to be a game changer; which meant he needed to have an "A Team" working on every product Apple sold. While I am sure Apple had a great staff at the time, Jobs knew that if the team was spread too thin, the result would be 350 products that were merely good, but not necessarily great.

Instead, he focused the efforts of the company and traded 350 good products for 10 industry- and society-changing products. The results could not be more stunning. Not only did Apple revolutionize the music business with the iPod and iTunes, but it also changed the way we work and communicate with the iPhone and iPad. More significantly, Apple is (at the time of this writing) the most valuable company in America. It is more valuable than

Exxon Mobil, and even more valuable than any bank or media company. The most valuable company in the country makes a relatively small handful of products, most of which did not exist only a few years ago. That is the power of focus.

The same focus can be applied to your life, business, or ministry. It doesn't matter what resources you have today; what matters is your ability to take those resources and focus them on whatever that thing is that you can do better than anyone else.

Another example of the power and ability to focus is In-N-Out Burger. This burger chain (which is probably my favorite) is based in California and is slowly expanding. What sets In-N-Out apart from the competition in the crowded fast food burger industry is its laser focus on a few great products. First of all, In-N-Out only sells burgers, fries, and drinks. In a world where the big players like McDonalds, Wendy's, and Burger King are constantly introducing products like salads, specialty lattes, and chicken, In-N-Out only does hamburgers and fries. The difference is that it makes those products very well—they only use fresh beef, the fries are made on-site (you can see them cut the potatoes), and they have great service. This company knows what they do well and they do that—and nothing else.

Can you imagine the focus required to build a large business based on such a simple concept? How many executives would have followed industry trends and added new products? How many executives would have wanted to abandon the company's policy of fresh, never frozen beef so that they could add more stores faster and impress Wall Street? Every time I wait in line to get an In-N-Out burger (I have to focus myself on not buying them too often), I am glad that the company stayed the course and kept its focus. The result is a great burger and a successful business.

An Honest Look

It is this ability to focus that is part of the challenge for church leaders today. It is time for leaders to take the resources they have, and channel them to achieve some real results. Let's get past having fake results for the sake of being able to say that we've got this or we've got that. We all love to say my church has 100 different ministries— we seem to have a ministry for everyone and everything. *We've got hundreds of ministries and isn't my church great?* we think to ourselves. Well, it may be great, but my question for you is this: Of those hundreds of ministries you have, how many actually work? How many of those ministries effectively change lives and influence people?

To bring focus, we need leaders who take an honest look at what their organization truly excels at. It's not whether or not you do it that's important; it's whether or not you do it *well*. And that's got to come from the top to provide that level of focus on what it is your ministry is and is not going to be about. It is up to the leadership to make those decisions. And then, once you know what it is your ministry is going to be known for, what the one thing is that you're going to be about, then you can build every-thing else around that one big idea.

You need focus because you're going to have many opportunities that come to you, and the question is, Do you have a filter so you can focus on what's important? Do you have a filter to pass all those opportunities through to help you decide where it is you are going to spend your time, money, and resources? Because at the end of the day that's what being a leader is all about. It is nothing more than making choices about how you spend your resources.

The fact is that you only have so many people who work for you or volunteer for you; you only have so much money in your budget. Every organization has finite resources that have to be allocated to specific places at specific times. Some organizations may be bigger than other organizations, but everybody has finite resources. So the question is, How do you focus those resources for effectiveness? As churches, I think we need to focus a lot less on the top line and a lot more on the bottom line. Sometimes it's not about how many people we bring into the doors; it's about how many people we are truly impacting, about the number of lives changed.

We need to have some real leadership in the church that's willing to step up and say, "You know, I understand that somebody in my church may not like it because maybe I'm going to cut out their ministry, but the fact is we're not doing it well. It's taking resources, and we need to focus on what we do well so that we can really impact the people."

The one challenge I have for you today as leaders is this: let's bring focus to the ministry. The laser-like focus will result in the relevance that we seek.

Focus on the Important, Not the Urgent

Another important aspect of focus takes place at the micro level. It is the focus that we bring every day to the office and to our lives. Just as a world full of distractions can cause an organization to lose focus, the same happens to us on an individual level.

We live in a world of constant emails, text messages, phone calls, endless meetings, and countless other distractions. As a result, it is all too easy to spend most of our time dealing with the situations right in front of us. However, just because you have 100 emails to answer doesn't mean that all 100 of those emails are important and should be answered in the same way. The problem is that we let the urgent take the place of the important.

One of the hardest things to do as a leader is to sort through all of the busy work in order to make sure that we continue to focus and make progress on the truly important matters that will have long-lasting impact. A lesson I have had to learn is that just because a certain matter is of top importance to someone else does not mean it has to be of critical importance to me. To be a truly effective leader, I need to focus on what is important to me, not on what others say is important and urgent.

To make my need to pay attention to what is important to me and the organization I run possible, while also being responsive and polite to all of the people vying for my attention, I have had to become much more blunt and up-front with those I interact with. In other words, focus requires that you become very good at saying no to certain things.

Just because an idea may be a good one or just because a business initiative may likely be very profitable doesn't mean it is right for you or your organization. The question is that after it passes through your filter, Is it right for you? But that question should come after it has already passed through your filter, not before going through your filter.

Bottom Line Focus

Another important aspect of focus is making sure that you are focused on the correct goals. All too often organizations focus on top line growth at the expense of what really matters, which is the bottom line. No organization can survive without a positive bottom line. However, many organizations focus instead on growing the top line without consideration of the cost to the bottom line. Blind focus on growing sales or growing church membership without consideration of the cost can cripple an organization.

I sit on the board of a company called Belief Net.com, which is one of the largest spiritual websites with about 4 million visitors a month. When our investment group bought this website a couple of years ago, the website had tremendous traffic but it was losing a lot of money. Once we did our due diligence and dug into what was really happening, we discovered that the prior management was buying traffic. Essentially, they were buying email names, using those names to drive traffic, and using the traffic numbers to sell ad space. The problem was that they were spending $1.50 to gain an additional $1 in revenue: a clearly unsustainable model. The prior management was focused on top line growth at the expense of the company's profitability.

When our management group took over, we immediately stopped this practice. The result was that traffic and ad sales started to decline. But even as sales went down, the losses were being eliminated and the company was headed toward profitability. Then we started to work on increasing traffic and ad sales without buying traffic. That is now happening and the website now has more traffic than it ever did, without the added expense. The bottom line focus led to the company actually having a bottom line.

Much the same thing happens in our lives, businesses, and churches. How many of us start to grow the top line (we bring home more money) only to allow our expenses to grow at the same time? The result is that there is no growth in the bottom line of the household. It order for our lives to be profitable, we must have a focus where the bottom line grows over the long run.

This top line focus also holds back many churches from growing the way God wants them to. There is too much focus on numbers—how many people were in church on

Sunday, how many visitors we had, etc.—and not enough focus on whether those people are actually involved, participating, and contributing. The real issue is our effectiveness in ministry—or is it just about a show that is put on for Sunday?

We need church leaders who will make the real thing the real thing. If it is just about the show, most churches will not succeed. That is not their gift. Instead, it needs to be about real outcomes—changing people's lives one at a time. This is why it is important to decide where your gift is, what you or your organization excels at, and focus on the big idea.

Long-term success will only come from implementing the big idea, having the ability to focus, and understanding the power of yes, which is our next characteristic we will examine.

Chapter 3

THE POWER OF YES

Just as learning to say no is critical to harnessing the power of focus in your organization, the uncommon leader also masters the ability to pull the trigger and say yes. In both business and in life, far too many people and organizations suffer from an inability of knowing when to say yes.

Reading the above paragraph, you may be thinking that I'm contradicting what I said in the last chapter about saying no. Didn't I just spend a considerable amount of time explaining how focus and the ability to say no is important? Yes, I did. One of the keys to organizational success is to focus on what you do best; and to maintain that focus you need to be able to say no to things you don't do well. However, at the same time, you have to be able to say yes to the right opportunities for success to come. Just as trying to do too much can hold you back, failing to act can keep you from the blessings God has for you.

Here are a couple of examples you may find familiar. The first scenario is what I call "waiting until the time is perfect" or "paralysis by analysis." This is the person or organization that simply can't make up their mind when a decision is presented to them. Think about the couple that has been engaged for years and still haven't set a wedding date. They may explain by saying things like, "We want to be more financially secure," or they want to wait until they are established in their careers. You may also hear similar things from people who say that they want to have children but have put it off for decades. In the business context, the leader is endlessly looking at financial projections, trying to judge the economy and make sure that every contingency is covered.

But the simple fact is that timing is *never* perfect. You can never eliminate all of the risks. Is it a good idea to exercise diligence, gather good information, and analyze options before making important decisions. However, good leaders get the information and then make a decision, whether right or wrong, and then move on to face the next set of decisions brought before them. But the truth is that people who never make a decision are in fact making decisions all the time. Their decision is to simply do nothing at all—not act at all.

Recently, my wife made two critical life decisions. After college, Julaina went to work for a private preschool. She loved the kids and the staff and parents, but didn't like the way the school was managed by the owners. So we got some partners (because we didn't have any money then) and bought the school she ran. After several years, the group of partners decided to sell the school. Julaina agreed to stay on and run the school for a while when the new owners took over. And a few years after that, the new corporate owners began to change the school in a way that diminished the experience the children received; so after almost 15 years of running the school, Julaina made the painful decision to leave.

She didn't have a plan about what to do next. She just knew God was telling her that she needed to make a change. So she left and started to enjoy more time with our kids over the summer. As the summer passed, however, she started to think about getting back to work (she is not one to stay home for very long). She also started getting calls from parents asking her to come back or start her own school. We then started to look at the options in front of us. I knew that the school she had been running was suffering without her in place. So, on a whim, I sent an email to the president of the company that owned the school and asked if he would consider selling. Yes, as a matter of fact, he was open to selling. We quickly agreed on a price (a lot less than we had sold the school for) and she is back in place, doing it her way and making the school a success once again.

When you are open and listening to what God is telling you, it is amazing what can happen in your life. My wife loves that school (sometimes I think as much as she loves me). It was incredibly difficult for her to listen to God and make the decision to leave. But she pulled the trigger and made the decision. She didn't wait until everything was perfect; but she acted on what God was speaking to her heart.

Then, just to show that God has a sense of humor, Julaina discovered that it was God's plan for her to be at the school, but now owning the school with no corporate owners to answer to. The plan was for her to have the school and be able to do it her way—the way God put in her heart. Moreover, our family will be financially blessed because now she keeps all of the profits. What a blessing for Julaina and our family, as well as the children, staff, and parents at the school—and all because she was willing to act.

God wanted Julaina to have the school, but first she had to listen. If she had played it safe and remained in place as director of the school, receiving a salary, she would still be there running the school. But she would still be frustrated by her lack of control and would not have the upside of ownership. It is clear, that by being open and willing to listen and say yes to God, you open yourself up to blessings that would never have come by just remaining comfortable and doing things as you've always done them.

It's Too Much Trouble

Another frequent refrain from people who don't act is, "It's too much trouble to do that." We all know people like this; they never venture outside of their comfort zone because it's too hard or will be too much trouble for them in some way.

While I may get in trouble for this example, my in-laws fall into this category. Don't get me wrong; they are nice people and good grandparents to my children. They are retired now and live on a little ranch in a small Texas town. They enjoy their cows, horses, and garden—that being the world to them.

We are not trying to get them to change their lifestyle at all. They enjoy life on the ranch and that is great. However, they could be such a larger part of the lives of their children and grandchildren if only they would open themselves up a little. I can't count how many times we have urged them, when they come to visit for a day trip, to stay over and spend more time with the family. The familiar refrain is, "No, we need to get home before dark," or "We need to feed the animals," etc.

The same thing happens when we try to get them to join us on trips. They don't want to be away from the animals for too long. I understand that they enjoy their life, but once you have experienced some of the great things God has provided in this world, you want to share it with those you're closest to. You want others to experience it. That is what we want for my in-laws—just to see what the world has to offer.

My wife and I have been extremely blessed. For a couple of kids from the Dallas suburbs, we live a pretty big life. We travel frequently and love spending time in Los Angeles and New York City. Because of my work as a film producer, we attend movie premieres and award shows. We have made a lot of good friends who happen to be famous for one reason or another. We love the ability to share this world with our family and friends. I like that we can take my niece, an aspiring actress, to a movie set and to the premiere of a movie. I hope that the experience will motivate her and allow her to see what is possible. Likewise, I know that my wife would love to show her mom around LA and enjoy an evening at one of our favorite places. My mother-in-law may not like New York or LA, and that is fine. But why not experience it just once? What if she found something there that truly inspired the rest of her life?

The point I am trying to make is that simply being open to opportunity can take you farther than you can ever imagine. I am a big believer that, as a parent, a businessman, and a leader, one of my responsibilities is to help others experience life. Why? Because the more you see, the more you see is possible; the more you see, the more you learn and can apply to your own life situations.

One of the best things my parents did for me was to make sure that I tried every activity as a child. From baseball to soccer to basketball to swimming to guitar lessons, I did it all at one point or another. Because of that broad exposure, I was able to find what I liked and had a talent for (which was competitive swimming). I think that leaders need to do the same thing with their teams, exposing them to as much as possible so they can grow thereby, becoming more effective leaders.

Exposure to Greatness Leads to Greatness

In my work consulting with church leaders, I am frequently astounded by how unfamiliar many church leaders are with what is going on in the broader church community. As a result, I encourage my clients and their leaders to get out and see what others are doing. Find a church that you have heard is doing great and go see what they are doing.

Why would I encourage them to do this? There are a lot of people who think they are doing well until they see how someone else is doing it. Next, I am a big believer in "clone and own." Simply put, if someone is doing something well, learn from it and adapt it to your own circumstances. In corporations around the country, people are constantly studying and learning from their competition—why not do the same thing in other environments?

No matter what it is you do in life, you need to be exposed to the very best in that field. It is only by exposure to the best that you can truly know where you stand. You may very well be the big fish where you live, but how do you compare to others? It is great to be the best swimmer in your country, but how will you do competing with the rest of the world in the Olympics?

The other advantage of being open and experiencing what others do is that you will make yourself better. If you live and work in an insulated world—meaning you always interact with the same people at work, at home, and at church—you are never stretched. Bishop Jakes is fond of saying, "If you are the smartest person in the room, you need to get into another room." Why? Because being around people who have knowledge and experience that we do not possess makes us better individuals. It stretches us. Getting out of your comfort zone is a good thing. However, it is not necessarily an easy thing to do. We all like our comfort zones. With coaching and leadership, though, you can build a culture where getting out of your zone is a positive and expected thing.

I have become so conditioned to being in new and different circumstances that I now actually crave it. If I had to do the same thing with the same people for too long, I would start to go crazy. I need the constant learning that comes with new situations, new environments, and fascinating new people.

So the power of yes is really all about being open and challenging yourself so you can go to the next level in your life, your relationship with God, and your leadership abilities. It has nothing to do with simply saying yes to every opportunity that comes your way. From a business and leadership standpoint, you need to maintain the focus that we have discussed above. But saying yes is about being open to the bigger world and what you can learn from it. Steve Jobs would not have been the executive who brought tremendous focus to Apple if he personally had not had such a broad life experience.

Moreover, I can absolutely affirm the same based on my personal experiences. I truly believe that one of my best assets, as a leader and as an executive, is my ability to draw on the breadth of my experiences. I have practiced law in both large and small firms, and I have experience working with publishers, music executives, and moviemakers. I interact daily with successful executives and business owners as well as actors, actresses, politicians, celebrities, and everyone in between. I have seen great sales people at work. I have seen creatives at their best. And I have also seen people at their worst. All of that experience makes me a better person. It means that whenever I have an issue to address, I can look to various industries for examples of how to address the issues at hand.

THE ENEMY OF LEADERSHIP

The benefit of opening up yourself to new people, new places, new experiences, and new ways of conducting business or living life is that it forces constant learning. When you live and work in an insulated world, you quickly reach the point where you are no longer challenged. I suppose that is what people like about such a life; they are comfortable.

To me, as a leader, that feeling of comfort is the enemy. When employees get too comfortable and too relaxed in their jobs, they lose their edge. Innovation stops. And worse yet, mistakes start to happen. Things become routine and we lose the ability to respond to a crisis.

Personally, being a surgeon or a pilot would be an incredibly difficult job. Yes, the jobs require a great deal of technical knowledge and skill—and I am confident that if I applied myself I could gain that knowledge and skill. To me the hard part is the routine of it all. The airline pilot who flies the same route on the same plane every day must find a way to remain vigilant and on edge despite having done the same thing thousands of times before. The same goes for the surgeon who has done the same procedure countless times. As the patient or the passenger, however, we want the surgeon or pilot who has the experience of having done it a thousand times to be the one taking care of us.

More importantly, we want the pilot or doctor who is ready to respond at a second's notice if something goes wrong. If you think about it, that is why the doctor or the pilot is paid what they are. It is not for the 1,000 times when everything went as planned; we pay them to be there and save the day when something goes wrong. That is why their jobs are so difficult. Most people cannot deal with that level of routine and still retain the edge needed for a crisis. That is why we don't want ourselves or our people to get too comfortable in what they do.

In some cases, there even a worse response by employees. When they get too comfortable, they begin to feel entitled. They are no longer making their best effort.

When apathy sets in, it can be hard to reverse. It is far better to continually show and expose your people to what is expected than to allow apathy to set in. Through varied experiences, your team will become continuous learners who see what is possible, thereby growing tremendously in the depth and vastness of their knowledge and experience.

At the end of the day, you cannot expect greatness from someone who has never been exposed to greatness. Routine exposure to greatness will benefit us as individuals, our teams, and the corporations or non-profits we are a part of. Then we will be able to create an experience for individuals that will give us our competitive edge.

Chapter 4

THE VALUE OF THE EXPERIENCE

One of the qualities of great organizations—from retailers to hotels to churches—is that they embrace and understand the value of "the experience." What do I mean when I talk about the experience? Whether a customer is visiting your retail store, a first-time visitor is attending your church, or a guest is staying at your hotel, everything that person sees, hears, touches, smells, and tastes is part of the experience that will remain with them long after they leave. The experience is both physical and emotional.

The experience begins with someone's first contact with you or your organization and extends through every moment of interaction and contact. The dress, disposition, attitude, friendliness, and responsiveness of every employee who has contact with a customer either contributes to or detracts from a positive customer experience.

You may be saying to yourself, Okay, I get it. To be successful you need to offer a good customer experience—everybody knows that. It's so obvious and simple. So, why does the topic deserve a chapter in a book on leadership?

The answer to me is equally simple, if not so obvious. Simply put, very few organizations implement positive customer experiences well. This is despite the fact that we all know it is important and we all give lip service to the idea of it. Virtually every company talks about their great service or high quality products or the importance of customers. So why is a truly great experience so elusive? It's because it is hard and requires leadership that understands the value of the experience (and how it fits for the business) and places an organization-wide emphasis on experience.

The main reason "the experience" deserves a chapter in this book is that it has a power that few leaders truly understand. Those leaders who truly get this concept and make it a part of the culture of their organization will quickly separate themselves and their organizations from the pack.

All of us can probably think of great examples of companies that provide a world-class experience. My go-to example is Disneyland. Our family has a tradition where every year we take one trip to Disneyland. Our family has been blessed that we can go, for the most part, anywhere we want to. So why, year after year, do we choose to spend part of our vacation time and money visiting Disneyland?

While there is a multitude of contributing factors—the rides are fun, the food is good, the entertainment is enjoyable—I have concluded that it is primarily about the experience itself. It is the sum total of everything that we do there. The park is impeccably clean, the staff (known as cast members) are always friendly, helpful, and in a good mood, and the background is uplifting. From the time we walk onto the Disney property and hear the music playing over speakers along the walkway, to the shopping and the dining and the parades and the shows, to the time we walk out at night, all contributes to a great experience. The end result is that everyone has a good time. While we all have our favorite things, it is always a positive experience for each of us.

Now think about the power of that "experience" from a business standpoint. First, the experience that Disneyland conveys to millions of visitors every year serves to consistently build and reinforce the Disney brand. My family and I feel great about Disneyland. As a result, we become repeat customers and we have spent a lot of money (I really do not want to know how much in total) at Disneyland. That means that Disney does not have to sell me to get me to come back. Any marketer or business owner knows just how expensive it can be to get new customers. When you can avoid or reduce that expense because of heavy repeat business, the contribution to the bottom line is significant.

So the power of the experience has made me a repeat Disney customer. But the power does not end there. Not only do I feel good about spending money at Disneyland, but I also tell other people how much my family likes Disneyland. Now I have become an advocate for Disneyland. I help Disney market its business.

Moreover, my positive Disneyland experience makes me feel good about other Disney products, like Disney movies. In other words, by delivering a great experience in one part of its business (theme parks), Disney builds its brand and helps its other businesses (such as movies).

One interesting note here: There are six major film studios—Sony Pictures Entertainment, Twentieth Century Fox, Warner Bros., Universal, Paramount, and Disney. Of these six majors, all of which are very well run companies and have existed for a long time, only Disney has a brand name that makes any difference to moviegoers. People will go see a Disney animated movie largely because it is a Disney movie—you know it will probably be good and that your kids will like it. On the other hand, whether Fox, Universal, or Paramount is behind a movie makes absolutely no difference to me in the decision to go see a movie.

Paying the Price for the Experience

But I want to discuss the real power of the Disneyland experience. Over the last decade I have spent thousands of dollars at Disneyland. In addition, I have spent lots of time in line waiting to get on a particular ride. I have shared the park, at times, with large crowds. But, at the end of the day, I don't care about the negatives—the crowds, the lines, the costs—it is still a great experience. Think about the power that represents from a business perspective. Because of the experience, Disney has built and reinforced its brand, made me an advocate for its theme park, and made its other products relevant. At the same time, the theme park itself is a great business because I happily pay a premium over and over again to visit the park. That is power.

It is power that works because from the top down, Disney knows that it is selling an experience. And that is what separates Disney from its competitors. By comparison, the Six Flags branded theme parks have long struggled to survive financially. The reason, I believe, largely boils down to the experience people get when they go there.

Six Flags, for example, has its Six Flags Over Texas Park about 30 minutes from my home. I grew up going to Six Flags and I loved it as a kid. Then, as an adult, I took my kids to Disneyland for the first time. There was no comparison in the quality of the experience. Once I had the opportunity to see there was something better, I was converted. Moreover, my kids were converted as well. They would much rather go to Disney once per year than have a season pass and go to Six Flags 20 times in a year.

On an economic level, the distinction is stunning. A 3-4 day pass to Disneyland costs about four times what a full season pass to Six Flags costs. Moreover, Six Flags is a 20-minute drive from my house. Disney is a three-hour plane ride away and requires a hotel stay. A couple of days at Six Flags would cost my family a few hundred dollars. A couple of days at Disneyland costs my family a few thousand dollars. Clearly, there is a huge economic difference in what it costs to go to each park. But, in terms of the actual rides (the heart of a theme park), many are largely the same. It is how they are packaged and the attention to detail that makes the difference for us. So a lot of elements are similar, and there is a huge difference in price; but we happily pay that price for the power of the experience.

The same concept applies to other companies and other businesses. In my view, one reason Apple is the most valuable company in America is that it understands it is not simply in the business of selling iPads and iPhones and Macs. Apple is selling an experience, a lifestyle. It is reflected in the design of the Apple stores, the people working in their stores (the Mac geniuses), the clean, simplistic design of their products, and how their products work. But it is all about an experience.

My wife loves Michael Kors, and he does a phenomenal job with his retail boutiques. His products (clothes, handbags, jewelry, etc.) are offered in other larger retailers. However, I much prefer to buy from one of his stores than from a retailer of his products. When I walk into one of those stores, I want to spend money because they treat you so well. They have beautiful models wearing the clothes that they're selling, just the right music is playing in the background, and it all goes to create an experience.

Michael Kors knows who his audience is and he creates an experience designed to cater to that audience.

I want to make an important distinction here. You may be thinking, *Well, of course Michael Kors can create this great experience; he must be selling ultra expensive products to wealthy women.* But in reality, he's not. While his products are not inexpensive (they are priced for upwardly mobile people), the products are not at all anywhere near the top of the market—it is a store for the upper middle-class. Even though he is not selling to wealthy elites (though I am sure many are his clients), he makes his customers feel as if they were. He gives the right experience for the right audience to create success.

And the same concept applies to Tiffany & Co., the jewelry chain. Over its history, Tiffany has carefully built an image of being the jewelry retailer for the rich and famous. Most people are familiar with the iconic blue Tiffany box. The stores are all located in the most exclusive shopping districts in each city they are located in (from Fifth Avenue in New York City to Rodeo Drive in Beverly Hills). The cases at Tiffany's highlight spectacular jewelry pieces costing, in some cases, hundreds of thousands of dollars. However, most people would be surprised to know that the average sale at Tiffany's is only a few hundred dollars. You see, Tiffany's has succeeded in becoming both a place where the few super-wealthy one-percenters can spend hundreds of thousands while the rest of us cumulatively spend a lot more money buying much less expensive items. Tiffany makes everyone feel special; and that is what sets them apart. Whether you spend $100,000 or $500, you get the same great experience.

Special Note for the Church

While we are on this subject of the experience, I want to convey a special message to churches and church leaders. Perhaps more than any concept discussed in this book, the experience is where churches can distinguish themselves from all others.

Think about what a church does and how it operates. The purpose of the church is to spread the gospel and help people lead better lives based on the model of Christ. But if you think about church from a business or economic perspective, there is a major point of distinction between a church and other organizations. While churches do "compete" for the attention of people, there is no "price" competition among churches. We do not make a decision on what church to attend for economic reasons (though I do think some people pick churches that can help them with their business, etc., but that is a subject for another discussion). All churches cost the same to attend. We pick a church because we enjoy going to the church. In effect, we like the experience it provides for us.

As someone who consults with and works with a lot of churches, it is amazing to me how little attention this gets. People just do things because they have always done them a particular way. As a result, many of the churches that are separating themselves from the pack, so to speak, are the ones that place an emphasis on the experience individuals receive once they drive into the parking lot.

We need church leaders who understand that it is not just about conveying the gospel, as important as that is. Consider for a moment the environment for churches today. I can get up on Sunday morning and stream the services of the biggest and best churches in America, all without getting out of my pajamas. I can watch great preachers on Christian television. I can read a book on a biblical topic that interests me. With all of these choices, why do I want to get dressed and go to your church? You better provide me and my family with an experience that I can't get at home. You have to be relevant, and good preaching alone is not what is going to get you there.

Church leaders today need to put an emphasis and priority on the experience. That means taking some lessons from Disney, Michael Kors, Four Seasons Hotels, and others. The best way, in my view, to think about the experience that your church offers is to look at it through the eyes of a first-time visitor. Imagine that you have never before been to your church. Walk through the experience from start to finish.

So often we become comfortable with our routine and our surroundings. We know and adjust to the quirks of a particular thing; we get accustomed to the negatives. Worse, we become insulated in our environment. Because we go to this church, we don't experience what others are doing (this is even worse for church leaders who, for the most part, have to be at their church every weekend). Just as I was satisfied with Six Flags until I experienced Disneyland, our church leaders have a false sense that they are doing a great job. They don't even know that the little church down the street is about to take over the town because they are, in fact, better.

The church experience starts in the parking lot. Is the lot well maintained? Are the volunteers working in the lot helpful and cheerful? Or, do you have a parking lot manager who takes his "authority" a little too seriously and irritates everyone who pulls in? Is there special help for first-time visitors? Go through the same process for every touch point a visitor has. Is it easy to find my way around? Does the service start on time? Does it end on time? What kind of experience do my children have? It all matters. The sermon alone is not enough.

Another important consideration is the web presence of your church. Perhaps I hear someone talking about your church and I am curious about it. The first thing I will do is look up the church online. The problem is, when I go to your website, I can't easily find your service times because they are buried five pages deep. I want to go to your church, but your own website makes it hard to get the information. The result is that I don't go.

Why do things like this happen? Because the website was put together by long-time members or staff people who are focused on the wrong things. They are focused on what matters to them, not to a newcomer. They know when service is and assumes everyone else does as well. They are not using the eyes of the first-time visitor.

In everything you do, think about the experience from the point of view of the people attending the church for the first time. Is it easy for them to find you? Is it easy for them to get information? How were they treated when they pulled in the parking lot? How were they treated when they walked in the door? And all of those things are a reflection of the leadership of the church. If there is an arrogant pastor, that will be conveyed throughout the church, and will most certainly be conveyed to a visitor. But if there is an open, receptive pastor, that's going to get conveyed to all who attend as well. As the pastor, as the leader, think about what it is that you are telling your people is important to you. The question is, Is that experience important to anybody else?

I like watching a show on television called *Restaurant Impossible*. These restaurant experts go into struggling restaurants that are about to fail and find the problems. Then they tell the owners how to fix the problems. I watched one episode and it was about two guys who had managed a restaurant together for 30 years. At one time, the restaurant was very successful; but over time it had declined and was about to go under, and the two owners were about to lose their life savings. As the experts dug into what was going on, they realized that the owners were creating an experience that was driving customers away. They had become very set in their ways and the restaurant had become about how they wanted it run—not about what customers experienced.

One of the owners would sit at home and watch the restaurant on his laptop via a camera system. For whatever reason, he didn't like it when someone would put something on the bar. He would be watching the camera, and seeing a customer put her purse on the bar, the owner would call the restaurant and have someone tell her to take her purse off the bar. Well, he may have gotten his way, but he also drove away a customer.

And so think about this in terms of your organization. What are you really trying to achieve? Is it really about you having things a certain way, or is it about you reaching people in an effective manner?

As a leader, how do you impact the experience that your customers or parishioners are receiving? Whether you know it or not, you are constantly sending messages to your staff about what is important to you. You are sending messages to your people and they are taking those messages and applying them—for better or worse. Consciously or not, all leaders clearly reward some behavior and discourage other behavior.

It is important to understand that you are the key to creating the experience. It is up to you, as the leader, to make sure that you're conveying the experience that you want others to experience. Whether you are leading a business, a school, or a church, it is incredibly easy for the leadership to get isolated. The pastor, like the CEO, has an assigned parking space and doesn't park where everybody else parks. You may not come in the same door everybody else comes in. The result is that you need to get out of your routine and view your business or church the way your customers view you. While it can be difficult as your organization grows, you still have to maintain that connection to understand things from the point of view of the person coming for the very first time and how they are being treated.

My wife, Julaina, has spent the last 20 years owning and running private Christian schools. One of the schools that she ran was located in a shopping center. It had a small playground and lacked many of the amenities that other competing schools had. So how did she compete, and do so successfully? She competed by delivering an experience. Her school didn't have all of the stuff, but it had the heart. People viewed the school as a family and they felt good about leaving their children in the care of her staff. Parents knew their children were learning, both academics and values. From a business standpoint, they also felt good about the investment they were making in their children's future.

Notice that I used the word investment in the last sentence. When parents are just getting someone to watch their children, they view that money as an expense. When parents know their children are learning, gaining values, and enjoying their time at school, now the money is an investment in the future, not an expense.

Our experience over the last several months has served to reinforce this point for us. My wife (together with some partners) owned the schools and ran them successfully for many years. As I said before, then a decision was made to sell to a large national chain. Julaina agreed to stay on to run the school and did so for a lot longer than she expected. Then, about a year or so ago, the company started to change how things were done. They put in place policies that kept Julaina in the office doing paperwork and not out doing what she was best at, which was spending time with the students. Recently, Julaina left the school along with many of her long-time staff and the school has lost many of its students. The new management didn't understand what made the school work.

For us, however, it is all working out. We are now buying back the school for a fraction of what we had previously sold it for. And this was all because someone didn't understand the value of the experience.

A Couple Additional Points

Before moving on, I want to make a couple of additional points about the power of the experience. Just as my wife was able to use a feeling and experience of family to offset other disadvantages that her school had, the power of the experience can be a differentiator in any business or organization. The experience someone has when they encounter your organization is what sets you apart from all of the other organizations, even if they offer more amenities than you do.

Movie theaters have been challenged over the last decade. The combination of ever-increasing quality of home theater systems and the decreasing time window between the theatrical release of films and release on VOD and DVD has left the theater industry struggling to find its relevance. Why go to the movies and pay for expensive popcorn and drinks when you can stay at home and get close to the same level of experience—all without buying tickets, waiting in line, or dealing with loud teenagers?

A couple of companies are finding ways to thrive in this environment by delivering a different type of experience. IMAX has succeeded by delivering an immersive experience for watching today's action-filled 3D blockbuster films. It is an experience that cannot be replicated at home, and true movie fans have flocked to it.

Another group has gone a different direction. AMC Theaters has a lot of traditional movie theaters, so they developed a concept that provides a completely different experience in the confines of a traditional theater. They converted some of their theaters to what they call "Cinema Suites." They took out every other row of seats and installed large, fully reclining leather theater seats. They offer high quality food and drinks delivered by wait staff. You even buy your tickets in advance online and get reserved seats, so you can show up when the show starts and still get the seat you picked. No one under 21 is allowed. My wife and I absolutely love it. And it is a great way to see a movie.

Both IMAX and Cinema Suites are examples of using a unique experience to overcome difficulties with a business model. These examples are particularly applicable to the church today. As we discussed before, many churches are struggling to find their point of relevance in a world where people have so many options. Just like IMAX and Cinema Suites, some are succeeding by intentionally creating a unique experience that cannot be replicated at home.

Another way that many churches are finding their relevance is by using the Disney model and creating an experience that caters to the entire family. More and more churches are spending significant portions of their budgets on children and youth. They know that by serving the children, they will serve the parents better, getting people who stay for the long term and commit to the mission of the church.

The bottom line is that if your organization is struggling, then focus on the experience you are delivering. If you were a first-time customer or visitor, would you come back based on the current experience? If not, what can you change to attract and retain more visitors?

Chapter 5

THE POWER OF THE BRAND

Once you have found and embraced the big idea for your business, church, or life, and you have brought a laser focus on what you do well, learn to say yes to great opportunities, and create an experience that no one will be able to forget, the next concept that naturally follows is the power of the brand. "Branding" is one of those buzzwords that business leaders, advertising executives, and consultants love to throw around. It is the topic of endless discussion and debate. We all talk about how every person and organization needs to brand themselves. While this is true, lets talk in practical terms about what this really means from the standpoint of the leader.

Since this is not a book on marketing or selling, but instead a book on leadership, let's focus on what the leader needs to know. On a high level, we all recognize what the value of a brand name is. The brand means you know what to expect from the product or service being offered. Whether it's a McDonalds Restaurant or a Four Seasons Hotel, you know what to expect from that particular brand. The McDonalds in New York is going to have the same Big Mac as the McDonalds in LA. The value for McDonalds is that they don't have to sell me again. I know what I will get when I go there. The one ad campaign works for all of the stores across the country.

From the standpoint of the leader, the brand question boils down to what your unique selling proposition is. Whether it is my wife's school, a church, or a billion-dollar business, every meaningful brand reflects the big idea (the unique selling proposition) that the organization is built upon. The question for the leader is whether you have established a brand or not.

The reason why many businesses and organizations do not capture the power of the brand is that they don't have one. There is no clear brand because there is no big idea steering the organization.

As surprising as it may seem, I think a lot of businesses and churches get started without any "big idea." Somebody just decided to be their own boss and started a business to do this or do that. They may even be enjoying a level of success, but there is no one big idea that sets them apart from their competitors, meaning the business succeeds based on their personal efforts. However, without the big idea and the power of the brand, it will not become something special.

Consider the nation's largest retailer, Walmart. From its inception, Walmart has been built on the single idea of being the one-stop shop, low-price mass retailer. Walmart got its start in rural America. Walmart's big idea was perfect for the business climate that existed in small town America in the 1960s and 1970s, which was mainly built on the mom and pop business model. There were shoe stores, grocery stores, a tire store, a music store, a craft store, etc. What Walmart did was combine all of these stores together in one larger store with the advantage of lower prices. Now whether you are a fan of Walmart or not (there has been a great deal of debate on the positive and negative impacts of Walmart on small town America), you cannot argue with its success.

When Sam Walton started Walmart in the 1960s, other retailers like Sears and Kmart were much larger and dominated the US retail scene. So why, 50 years later, is an upstart retailer from Bentonville, Arkansas, the nation's largest retailer while Sears and Kmart have struggled and are now one company fighting to survive? While I am sure there are a myriad of business decisions that led to the decline of Sears and Kmart, one glaring issue to me is that they lack the power of the brand. There is not one big idea that is central to either company; they lack an identity.

A big part of Sears has always been about hardware and other durable hard goods (like appliances and tires).

However, their mall-based locations are too inconvenient to be a first choice for me when I need a specific tool or am shopping for a new appliance. But Sears has recently started a clothing line with the Kardashians, of which I'm a fan (it is one of my guilty pleasures). But, for the life of me, I cannot see what the connection is between the Kardashians and Sears. No one (especially the young female fans of the Kardashians that Sears is hoping to attract) believes that the K sisters would ever shop at Sears. I may be wrong, but it seems like a combination of two inconsistent brands. I do, however, tip my hat to Kris Jenner for what must have truly been a masterful sales job.

On the other hand, Macy's has built an incredible marketing and branding campaign built around a wide variety of celebrities. The commercials feature celebs such as Martha Stewart, Donald Trump, P. Diddy, Justin Beiber, Jessica Simpson, and Emeril. Each one of the celebrity brands highlighted in the Macy's ad campaign represents quality, style, and the best. Their products are at Macy's and the result is very inspirational. The point is that the marketing reinforces the brand message that the company is trying to convey.

CLARITY OF THE BRAND

Whether it is your personal brand, your company's brand, or the brand of your ministry, it must be simple and clear in order to be effective. In other words, you need brand clarity. You and everyone else in the organization must know what the brand is and how it relates to the big idea at work in your company.

One of the best examples of brand clarity is Coca-Cola. I have been in a number of meetings with executives at Coca-Cola—everyone there is very clear. Coca-Cola equals happiness. That simple sentence and thought is what the company is built around. It seeks to convey that message in all of its advertising. "Have a Coke and a smile," reads the caption on the familiar Christmas commercials with the polar bears, making you remember a time of happiness in your own life, associating Coke with that thought.

With many organizations, you will find anything but clarity of the brand. In my work with churches, I frequently ask what the one thing is that this church is known for. In virtually every case, I will get as many different answers as people I ask. It is each person's idea of what makes the church good—the teaching, the preaching, the Sunday school, etc. What does that tell me? To start, it means that the top leadership has not conveyed what the big idea is, if they even have one. Usually, there is no real idea that is being pursued. It is something like, "We want to be the best church we can be and represent Christ." That is a nice thought, but how are you going to do that? What sets you apart? What is the big idea?

When you can answer those questions, then you can begin to build a brand with some clarity. Without that clarity, you are just another church. You may do good things, but you will be unlikely to rise to the level you are seeking.

The power of focus must be applied to the big idea to help you form a brand that is easily communicated to your staff, leaders, and employees. The brand, in effect, begins to act as a filter to help you decide what to do and not do. At TDJ Enterprises, our mission is to educate, empower, and entertain; so everything we do has to fit the overall T. D. Jakes brand and mission. We are clear on what this represents. So when we evaluate one of the many proposals we get every day, we can ask, "Does this fit the brand?" It may be a wonderful idea; it may be a great business; but the question is whether or not it furthers the brand, or whether or not it's something we think that we can excel at. Does it fit our mission? So we have a filter through which we focus what we're going to do. Otherwise we're going to drown in a sea of opportunity.

So no matter what we are doing, we must clarify what makes us unique, what sets us apart, and what makes us different from our competitors. We don't want to be just another organization filling up office space; we want to be an organization that makes a difference in the lives of individuals and the world. And for that to happen, we must develop and clarify our brand.

Chapter 6

Make a Great Trailer (a.k.a. the Elevator Speech)

While I did not realize it at the time, I got a great leadership lesson while I was in law school. Professor Bill Dorsaneo is both a legal genius and the teacher nobody wants. Most students didn't like him because he spent less time talking about what you, as a student, needed to know and most of the time talking about what he was interested in. As a result, he wasn't the best teacher if you wanted to understand what was going to be on the final exam. He was, however, incredible if you wanted to really understand the law. I may be the only person in history who took four of his classes and was his research assistant.

At the end of the day, my willingness to do what most people viewed as difficult yielded great results. At one point, I was giving thought to becoming an appellate lawyer (I could envision myself arguing cases before the Supreme Court). So I took Dorsaneo's appellate practice course and got a great lesson that I want to share with you.

When you draft an appeal of a case, you are basically, in written form, explaining what the lower court did wrong (or right depending on what side you are on) and why your client should win. Professor Dorsaneo, in addition to teaching, has a very successful appellate practice. He also takes a very different approach to appeals than most lawyers.

Most lawyers like to list every possible error that the trial court made and every possible reason why their client should win. They think the longer the brief, the better it is (probably because they get paid by the hour). Dorsaneo, on the other hand, had a very different approach. He explained to us that the justices who would be reading the brief were real people. That means they are busy; they have families and responsibilities just like everyone else. As such, he explained that you have to assume that the justice will be reading your brief on a sofa while his five-year-old watches cartoons. In other words, he was saying that you couldn't assume that the justice will give your brief his or her undivided attention. We needed to assume the reality that our audience was distracted and tired. Therefore, instead of the throw everything against the wall and see what sticks approach, Dorsaneo taught us that we needed just *one* reason why we should win. Keep it simple and help the justice do his or her job—that is how you win.

This approach has benefited me so much in life. Whether it is law, business, or life, at the end of the day the way you win arguments or get people to follow you (sounds like we are back to leadership) is to have a clear, simple reason for your position.

MAKING GOOD TRAILERS

Much later in life, and in a much different circumstance, I essentially got the same lesson. As I have mentioned, one of the great benefits of opening yourself up and putting yourself in new situations is that you inevitably end up learning something you can apply in your life. A few years ago, I had one of those experiences. Bishop Jakes and I were in Los Angeles for a series of meetings at Sony Pictures. We were in the process of selecting a director for our film *Jumping the Broom*. We had flown in from Dallas that morning and we were the first to arrive at the meeting. While we were waiting on Tracey Edmunds and Glendon Palmer, our producing partners, and Elizabeth Hunter, the writer, to arrive, Devon Franklin, who is a Sony executive, walked into the room with Will Smith.

We had all met previously when we had partnered with Sony to help promote Will's film *The Pursuit of Happyness*. As we talked, Will asked what we were working on and then he gave us some of the best advice I had ever heard. "Don't ask the director about the movie that he's going to make for you," he said. "Ask the director about the trailer, because, as the most successful actor in Hollywood, I have learned that I am not in the movie making business. I'm in the trailer making business." The more I thought about it, the more that simple piece of advice stuck with me. And I have repeated that story over and over because Will Smith's advice not only applies to the movie business, but it also applies to life and business in general.

What Will Smith was saying is that people make a decision about whether to go see a movie based on the two-minute trailer, not based on the entire movie. As a result, you can make an incredible film, a sure Academy Award Winner, but if the trailer does not do a good job of conveying the message that sells the film, it won't matter. Those people sitting in the theater watching the previews will not be talking about how they want to see that movie when it comes out. They will forget they saw the preview and the movie is likely to be equally forgotten.

While it is easy to understand why the trailer is so important to the success of a movie, let's talk about how the same idea applies to your life and your business or ministry. Just as people do not make a decision to see a movie based on the entire picture, people do not make a decision about whether to work with you, follow you, or partner with you based on the whole of your life. Instead, the trailer concept applies to the individual. We make judgments about people and organizations based on a very short trailer. We don't have the benefit of knowing someone's life story until we have spent a lot of time with that person. We decide who we want to be around based on initial impressions and interactions.

One big distinction is that trailers are made "on purpose" by professionals who watch the whole movie repeatedly and pull out the best parts to show the world. Have you ever gone to a movie and left thinking that all of the best parts were in that two-minute trailer? That is what happens when a great trailer cutter works on a bad film. If only two minutes were good, they will find those two minutes and include them in the trailer.

In life, however, most of us don't even realize that we are walking, talking trailers for ourselves and the organizations we represent. As a result, we are very often not showing the world the best of what we have to offer. Whereas, as leaders, once you become aware of the importance of the trailer, you can begin to build yours "on purpose."

Think about this concept in the context of a church. When your congregation leaves your church on Sunday and they go to work on Monday, what is the trailer they're playing to their co-workers? How about in the way they live their lives? In the way they conduct themselves? In what they say about what you said on Sunday? Your congregation is going out every Monday and running the trailer from last Sunday, which is the trailer for next Sunday for you and your church. People all over your city are making decisions about whether or not they want to take the time and the energy to come to your church based on that trailer.

The pastor and leader of the church may never meet or interact with the many people that members of the congregation influence every week. However, all of those people (who the pastor has never met) are making judgments and decisions about whether to attend that pastor's church based on the "trailer" or "elevator speech" that a member of the congregation created and conveyed to his co-workers. If that member is a great person, who is positive and always has great things to say about church, the pastor, and what he or she learned, that will have a positive impact on the people around that member. Their co-workers will naturally become curious about something that has had such a positive impact on the person they know. Likewise, the reverse is also true. People who are negative and always complaining about the parking at church or the sermon being too long are going to negatively influence their co-workers.

The same concept applies to us as individuals. We all need to become intentional about the messages that we put out to the world. How you dress, how you speak, how informed you are, how you present yourself—it is all about the trailer that is your life.

If you really want to make a difference in your life, spend some time thinking about the trailer that your friends, family, and colleagues are viewing about you. What is the message that you are trying to send? Does your manner of dress say, "I don't care," or does it say, "I am classy and confident"? Make a list of all of the negative traits about you that are being conveyed by your "trailer." At the same time, make a list of all of the positive things that you want to convey, and note whether or not your "trailer" gets the point across. Based on these lists, you can start the process of editing your personal trailer.

Again, the same applies to your business also. When you go into the office tomorrow, take some extra time to look at everything through the eyes of a first-time client or customer. How does the receptionist treat people? What do your offices say about you? Does your website and other marketing materials convey the right message? If not, what can you change to make those things convey the right message?

Remember, while you can't do anything about the message that you put out yesterday, you can always edit and fix tomorrow's message. You just need to take the time and think about the messages you are sending. And be intentional about what you want to say. The way that trailer that is played out to world is one that is positive, causing people to want to look into what you're offering because you're trailer is so good.

THE ACTIVE CHOICES

So far in this book, I have been focused on what I would call the purely mental aspect of uncommon leadership. One of my frequent refrains is that life is cumulative. Everything we do and think adds up to a result. More often than not, it is not the big decisions that determine success in life, it is the millions of small, seemingly insignificant decisions and actions (and inactions) that add up to the result.

The concepts I have discussed in the previous chapters—recognizing and embracing the big idea, choosing to focus, being open to yes, harnessing the power of the brand, and understanding the significance of making a great trailer—have all been about the multitude of mental choices we make every day that add up to leaders and organizations exemplifying those traits.

I want to now move on to a series of more action-oriented characteristics displayed by uncommon leaders: building a foundation, getting a coach, understanding the power of the team in order to win, and understanding and acknowledging what we don't know to fill in our information gaps. Then I'll tie it all together in the last chapter.

Chapter 7

Building the Foundation: Making the First Thing the First Thing

The ideas and concepts in the first section of this book are about the choices that separate the special leaders and organizations from the others. Big or small, if an organization reflects the choices discussed in the first section, the seeds of something special have been planted. However, there is also a more practical, active side to the choices that leaders need to make.

The first is that the leader has to set out to establish and build a proper foundation; regardless of whether it is for a business, a church, or an individual life. You have to build a strong foundation or else when you finally take that big idea, focus on it, and build a great brand, the weight of the success will cause you or your organization to crater. In this chapter I want to discuss a few choices and actions that leaders can take to build the needed foundation.

Just as you need to be ready to embrace the big idea, you also need to think big even when you are just getting started. No matter the size or the scope of your organization today, one of your biggest challenges and mandates as a leader is to think big even when you're not. Why? Because wouldn't it be a tragedy if you put this book down today, went to bed, and woke up tomorrow and God gave you the big idea, and then he gave you the platform to put it out there, but you weren't ready because the foundation wasn't laid? The pathway to meaningful success is littered with people and organizations that simply weren't ready when the opportunity came.

We have a tendency to underestimate what God can do and, as a result, we tend to think that we can do the hard work of getting ready after success has already happened. The problem is that once you hit a certain level of success, you are going so fast that you have to rely upon what you have already built because you don't have time to build an infrastructure. When success happens, the infrastructure already needs to be in place.

This is why you see so many tragic stories about young and immensely talented athletes and entertainers who have so much difficulty managing a life of apparent success. When you go straight from school to stellar fame and financial success, it can be very difficult to build an infrastructure on the fly. It must be built before success comes.

Likewise, the same applies to organizations, both businesses and churches. The business that grows too fast is just as likely to have financial difficulty as the one that doesn't grow at all. When the infrastructure is not in place to manage people and products and processes, mistakes begin to happen, contracts go unfulfilled, and customers become unhappy. When you spend all day every day just trying to catch up, you can't embrace the concepts in this book—you can't think at all. You just have to act and that rarely leads to a good result.

In the last presidential election, for example, businessman Herman Cain ran for the Republican nomination. He didn't have any political experience, but as the primary races began to heat up he surged in the polls after the fifth or sixth Republican debate. Then, just as quickly as he surged, his campaign came to a halt after allegations of sexual harassment. So why is this story relevant? Because we all know that nobody pays attention until you are out front, but once you become a winner, the scrutiny begins. The problem for Cain is that he clearly wasn't prepared to manage the scrutiny of being a front runner. Had Mr. Cain built his infrastructure at the beginning (on the assumption that he would get to the head of the pack), he would have had the right team and the right answers in place. He would have been able to manage the assault from the press.

As the Herman Cain story illustrates, success is exponentially harder than failure. With success comes scrutiny, pressure, and people pulling at you from every different direction. You need to have a team of people you can trust before you get there. After you are there, you can never know what is motivated out of friendship and respect and what is motivated because of money and position. And that is something that you have to be ready for, which means you have to build your structure for it now before you ever become successful.

ORGANIZATIONAL FOUNDATIONS

Organizations, even those that exemplify many of the qualities discussed in Section One, also have to think big if they want to get big. At the beginning of the fast food hamburger craze in America, two brothers were extremely successful. Their restaurants were very profitable and they had great systems in place. They offered a good product at a decent price and they made a great deal of money.

However, what they couldn't do was expand their vision beyond a few locations. When the restaurant caught the attention of the man who sold them their milkshake machines, that all changed. That man was Ray Kroc and he had the vision to take the hamburger chain around the world. Mr. Kroc was a big thinker. He knew that the McDonald brothers had a great concept but lacked the vision and the foundation to grow the hamburger chain. Ray Kroc bought McDonalds and the rest, as they say, is history.

The McDonald brothers were great at operating a restaurant. What they couldn't do was replicate themselves. As long as they were involved in the business, it worked. What Ray Kroc was able to do was to think big, build the foundation, and create a restaurant that could be replicated without having a Ray Kroc or a McDonald brother there to run it. By building the foundation and the system, Kroc could take a great idea (which the McDonald brothers had run with a great deal of focus) and make it grow. Had the McDonald brothers continued to own the restaurants that bear their name, it is likely that most of us would never have had the pleasure of a Big Mac!

Regardless of whether it is a business or a ministry, to grow you have to build the foundation first. Before you go up, you have to dig down into the ground and lay a proper foundation that will support the weight of your success. The structure will not stand the weight of success if the proper foundation hasn't been laid.

In business terms, this means developing systems, building a team, and delegating. You see, without the foundation, you can only build as far as the leader can go. But with the right team and systems in place, you can grow without limits, just how God has planned for you.

Another vital element of building your foundation is doing the hard work and having substance. As an individual, this means having more than sizzle, more than a great presentation. It means being able to back it up. If you are in ministry, it means knowing your stuff, being able to get beyond the platitudes and getting to the substance. But you have to do the work, which is oftentimes hard.

From our churches to our politicians to our business leaders, we have far too many "leaders" who look the part (they look great in the suit) and act the part (they know all the right buzzwords to say), but at the end of the day there is no substance. When the weight of the organization starts to bear down, those without the substance, who haven't done the work, will crumble.

One of the unfortunate side effects of capitalism is that sometimes you can succeed (or at least make money) by being in the right business at the right time and benefiting from a great marketplace. However, it is the ability to survive long-term that separates those with substance who have done the work from those who have sidestepped many of the foundational elements that should have already been in place.

You need some substance, and that means you've got to take the steps now to get yourself ready for what's coming. You've got to properly structure your organization for success. You've got to build your team. You've got to understand all those things that we talked about in this chapter and implement them. You've got to understand branding, you've got to understand coaching, and you've got to be able to put all this together and have the proper focus for your organization.

To be successful you've got to be able to bring all these things together to have the proper foundation before you can even think about getting to the point of success. But with the right foundation in place, when success comes, you'll have everything in place and be able to be profitable.

Chapter 8

EVERYONE NEEDS A COACH

As I am writing this chapter, it is August 2012 and one of my favorite things happening right now is the Summer Olympics. My wife, children, and I are glued to the television every day during these games. Two weeks straight of watching the opening and closing ceremonies, the swimming, gymnastics, track and field, boxing, basketball, and everything else are truly exciting. My wife even has the Olympic app on her iPad so that she can stream the events in real time, not having to wait for them to air on television.

So what do the Olympics have to do with a book on leadership? If you think about it, the Olympics are a competition among the very best athletes in the world at what they do. Whatever their respective sport is, the Olympians are the very best in the world, each representing the finest of their country. And every one of those athletes has something in common—a coach. Every single athlete at the Olympics has one or more coaches.

Gabby Douglas may be the best gymnast on the face of the planet. Nobody else can do what she can do. And nobody can swim faster than Michael Phelps in his events. Even though they are the best at what they do, Michael Phelps and Gabby Douglas both have a coach. Phelps's coach cannot swim faster than he can, but he's critically important to Phelps's success and training.

Let's take a second and think about why a good coach is so important to overall success. If you are the best in the world at what you do, why do you need a coach? Can you really get that much better?

Human nature is incredibly difficult for us to self-evaluate. So the coach has an advantage of being able to watch an athlete's performance with a critical eye. Because the athlete is focused on the competition at hand, or even the practice, it is the coach who watches, observes, and notices the small details that will help the athlete improve his or her performance. The sum total of all those observations add up to make an athlete even better.

I happen to have been a swimmer when I was in high school, and so I love swimming. I remember at the 2008 Olympics when Michael Phelps was going for seven gold medals in a single Olympics. For him to get one of those gold medals, he had to be on a relay team that had to win. I will never forget that race; they won it by $1/100^{th}$ of a second. Yes, the athletes had to perform that day as best as they ever had before. Largely, however, such a close race was won as a result of coaching. It was the result of all those little suggestions and hints that happened in training. All those little things that a coach suggested and that an athlete implemented added up to make that team $1/100^{th}$ of a second faster.

Another reason that coaches are important is that they motivate. To see the importance of motivation, look at professional sports. Surely, if anyone should be self-motivated it should be professional athletes. You have teams largely made up of multimillionaires who get paid to play sports at the highest level possible. Surely, we think, an athlete being paid $10 million or $20 million a year to play baseball doesn't need any motivation. But we would be wrong.

Why then are great coaches so sought after in professional sports? It is because they can motivate even the best athletes to do even better. As anyone who has excelled at anything knows, it is incredibly hard to perform at a high level day after day. But coaches are there to give hints, tips, and tricks to improve performance on a consistent basis.

This same principle applies to everyone, not just athletes. If you do anything for a long period of time (no matter how much you enjoy it or how much you get paid to do it), it can become a grind. Whether you are a pro baseball player who plays 162 games in six months, an actor doing eight performances a week on Broadway, or a pastor doing four sermons a weekend, it is tough to perform at your highest level on a consistent basis. That is where a coach comes in. The coach helps you work through the inevitable ups and downs. They can notice when your performance starts to change and get you back on track. And a good coach knows when to push you and when to leave you alone.

Coaches also bring the value of their experience to the table. Because the coach has very often been there and done that, he or she can offer the wisdom that they have gained over time. Either as a coach or when they were a player themselves, coaches have often been down the path that the athlete is trying to go down. That means the coach can help the athlete avoid mistakes that perhaps they made while they played the sport.

And because of their more extensive experience, the coach can help with the decision-making process when it comes to performance. "You should do this, but don't do that," they instruct their players. They can help us know when to push ourselves and they know when we need some rest; when we just need to relax and when we need to get amped up.

In team sports, in particular, which have the most in common with organizational dynamics, the coach plays another crucial role. They put together the game plan for the entire team. Why does the coach do this and not the quarterback? After all, the quarterback has to go out and execute the game plan. The reason is simple: it takes the entire team to execute the game plan. That means that the coach, the person who sees what everyone does and what everyone can do, organizes a plan that maximizes the strengths of the team and minimizes their weaknesses. Coaching is more than simply motivating someone to be better, it is also thinking and planning to get the most effective result out of the team.

For the all reasons we have discussed, we prize and hold in high regard great coaches—Tom Landry of the Dallas Cowboys; Phil Jackson and Pat Riley from their LA Laker years; Bear Bryant at Alabama. At the same time, we are quick to blame the coach when our favorite team loses.

Finally, great coaches know their athletes, and know them well. Every sport, no matter how physical, has an arguably more important mental factor. As a result, coaches have to learn and understand what makes every member of their team tick. We are all motivated by different things. We all have different levels of mental toughness, discipline, desire, and other "intangibles." We need our coach to understand who we are and help us play to our strengths and compensate for our weaknesses.

THE VALUE OF COACHING

It doesn't matter if you run a multibillion dollar business, a church, or a football team, great coaches and leaders understand the mental part of the game and the mental aspects of their team members. The question is, If we realize how valuable coaches are in the world of sports, why do we think coaches have no place outside of sports? That is one of the biggest mistakes we make in the business world.

Whether it is a large multinational corporation, a church, or a local restaurant, every organization needs leaders who value coaching.

If we want our organizations to improve, we need leaders who are willing to coach and encourage others to do the same. We also need employees who have been shown the value of coaching and are willing to accept good coaching. For coaching to be effective, it has to be a two-way street.

As a leader, one of the most important characteristics I look for in employees is attitude. Why attitude? Because if someone has a positive attitude and is willing to become more than they are, they are coachable. People with a negative attitude, however, don't want criticism (no matter how it is delivered) and can't be coached.

So how then do you instill an attitude of coaching and being coached in your organization? Simple: the leader has to start getting coached and start coaching others. It takes both to be truly effective in leadership. If you want your people to value your coaching, show them that you are being coached and are better for it. You, as the leader, need to be humble enough to recognize that you can be better than you presently are. It is not a sign of weakness to seek help and get it.

Everyone, no matter what your position, needs to find one or more mentors or coaches who can motivate you, occasionally criticize you, and push you to be a better person and become better at what you do. If you take the view that you are above coaching, that will quickly filter down to your organization and you will have a hard time coaching others.

Special Note for the Church

Like world-class athletes, it wouldn't be hard to motivate pastors and others in leadership in churches—they just need a coach. After all, you are working for the best cause in the world. You truly believe in what you are doing. Maybe that is why most church leaders don't reach out and get the coaching they need—maybe they think it is a sign of weakness or that they are less than fully dedicated to Christ and his cause.

However, as we discussed, coaching is not only about motivation. It is also about experience, knowledge, making good decisions, and providing positive criticism. Church leadership needs to move past its issues and embrace the need for coaching. Why? Because it makes us better. Church leaders have a critical mission and they need to be effective. And coaching can move that process forward.

It is because of this need for coaching that Bishop Jakes offers multiple events a year for pastors and church leaders. It is why I wrote this book. It's why I am the president of Ascension Advisory Group, a company formed with a simple purpose: to advise churches and leaders, and to help them become more effective at what they do. While our services may take the form of public relations help, branding, or marketing, at the end of the day it is really about acting as coaches for our clients. We want to share with our clients the knowledge, experience, and wisdom that we have hopefully gained over our careers.

For some reason, there is a mindset in the church world that people think they should do everything themselves. There is a reluctance to accept coaching and mentoring. Like I said before with Michael Phelps, his coach is not important to him because the coach is better than him; the coach just has a unique insight on what it takes to make him better. That is what coaching is all about—you becoming a better individual. It's not taking something away from you. It's not weakness for you to accept coaching. And we need our leaders to step up and recognize that and to find coaches.

I have been blessed to have a number of mentors and coaches in my life. They are people who have had different and better experiences in some areas than I have had. I look to them as my coaches because maybe they can see something a little bit differently than I can; maybe they've been down a road that I haven't been down yet. We need that acceptance of the value of coaching for our churches. We need that to be able to move things forward in a different way because we can't go where we haven't been before if we don't have the benefit of somebody who has been down these paths before. That's why you call a trailblazer a trailblazer. You need somebody, if they've been down that path before, who can help guide your path and help you along the way. So we need to start looking beyond ourselves and find other resources to help us.

You need to find in your life those coaches who can help you to become better; people who have a different perspective and a different experience level than you. The added value will be immense, both to you and your team. Then your job as the leader is to become the coach to your team. So the leader needs his own coach and the leader needs to become a coach in order to truly be effective.

A quick side note here: Biographies can act as virtual coaching tools. To be successful, you need to expose yourself to people who have achieved success. One simple way to do this is to study successful people through what they write, and through what's written about them.

One of my favorite autobiographies is *Winning* by Jack Welch, who was the long-time CEO of General Electric (widely considered to maybe be the best chief executive ever). In reading his story, it struck me in the book that he said he spent 25 percent of his time with the leaders in his company. A quarter of his time was spent with the people underneath him, making them better executives so that they would do a better job of running their respective departments, ultimately moving up within the company.

This is an example that needs to be followed. Jack Welch knew that General Electric could not maintain long-term growth and success without developing a steady stream of great executives to run the company's far-flung businesses. So if you envy GE and its long-term success, you should follow Jack's advice and focus on developing your people.

One of the things that will happen when you get a coach and you become a coach to the people in your organization is that everyone will become better for it. You will also be in a better position to perform another critical duty of coaches, which we haven't yet discussed. In addition to making people better, coaches are also charged with finding the best position for each person.

In order to make the team or the organization as good as it can be, each player has to be in the right position. One of your jobs as a leader in that organization is to help make everybody else better. A great athlete or employee is not going to reach their potential if they are cast in the wrong position. It is up to the coach to find the best position for everyone within, maximizing effectiveness for the greater good.

Recently, I was talking about this topic at a pastor's conference. One of my good friends, Bishop James Dixon of the Community of Faith Church in Houston, was in the audience. As I was making this point, I had to break the news to Bishop Dixon that he was not going to be the starting quarterback for the Houston Texans. He just isn't the best man for that job. Putting him in that position wouldn't serve anyone involved. If Bishop Dixon was the quarterback of the Texans, the Texans wouldn't win any games and Bishop Dixon likely would not survive the process. The same would likely happen if we made Matt Staub the pastor of Community of Faith.

However, if we get the right people in the right positions, we are ready to maximize our results. So think of yourself in that role of coaching a team. You are responsible for deciding how to deploy that team, who the starters are, and who's on the bench. You decide who needs extra practice and who is ready to start the game.

The last function that a coach provides may be the most important of all. The coach makes the team a team. Without the coach, most teams are just a group of individuals who could easily do their own thing. It is the coach who gets the group to work together, who gets each individual to perform at his or her best so the team is successful. And it is the coach who decides who should play what role on the team. They motivate and keep the team focused on a common objective.

If you are ready to lead, you need to be ready to spend a lot of your time coaching those around you. Some people would lose with your team, but others would win with the same team. The difference is the coach.

Chapter 9

IT TAKES A TEAM TO WIN

Closely related to the concept of coaching is the importance of the team. If there is one thing holding back many organizations today, it is that they have forgotten the importance of the team. No one person, no matter how talented they are, can do it all for any real period of time.

It takes a whole team working together in concert toward a common goal and objective to achieve lasting and meaningful success in any endeavor. From a business standpoint, I have learned a great deal about the importance and proper functioning of an effective team from my work in the film business. In the course of my career, I have produced five feature films. No other endeavor that I have been involved with has been as collaborative as film production. As a film goes from idea to script to prep to actual filming to post-production to marketing, the process involves a constantly changing group of team members, many of which never see or work with each other.

At the beginning of the process, the team is small with just the producers, the writer, and the studio executives. Later, after there is a script, the team then expands a little and the director is added to the team. Then a casting director is then added and then the cast is added to the team. When you get ready to start making the team, its size explodes as you add crew, the rest of the cast and extras, etc. Finally after filming is done, the team shrinks again to only a few people—the director, the editor, the producers, the studio executives, and the post-production team that add music, etc.

So as a producer, one of the main jobs is to assemble and manage this large and constantly evolving team of professionals. Today, the people who do most of the work making films simply go from project to project. There is very little continuity between productions. This means that a group of people, who for the most part have not worked together, need to come together, understand their common goals and objectives, get along with each other, and get the work done in a high pressure environment.

Having gone through this process several times, there are a few lessons that have stood out to me. One lesson is that effective teams always collaborate. As you can imagine, filmmaking is a creative process. To end up with a quality film, the various members of the team have to collaborate effectively. To accomplish a scene that meets the director's vision, multiple creative groups must work together. The hair and makeup team have to create a look that works with wardrobe, the art department has to create a set that matches the director's vision, the props have to be in place, etc. And it goes on and on.

How can so many people, without a history together, collaborate so effectively? It's simple: they have professionalism. The various creatives on the team all contribute their viewpoint and opinion in a professional manner. Yes, people are passionate (they are artists) and they advocate for their view, but once the decisions are made, they get on board and give their best effort. For the team to function effectively, people can't take disagreements personally. Members say what they think, a decision is made, and then you get on with the work at hand. The ability to do this comes from the producer, the one in charge of it all. If the leaders set the right atmosphere for effective collaboration and discussion, the team will largely follow.

One of my favorite examples as this type of interaction among a staff or team comes from the long-running television series *The West Wing*. For those of you not familiar with the show, it stars Martin Sheen as the President of the United States and the show, for the most part, is a drama that follows the day-to-day workings of the president's staff. Many of the episodes feature vigorous and full-throated debate of issues among the staff members. The purpose of the debate is to aid the president in his decision-making process. The ability to engage in spirited debate and keep it professional is critical to a fully functioning team. If your team can't have a vigorous debate and then go out to lunch together, they can't get the best of what your team has to offer.

Remember, each member of your team has a perspective and outlook that is unique to them as individuals. That means no one else will have quite the same viewpoint on any given situation. As the leader, you need to encourage your team to argue passionately for their position. Then, when the debate is over and the decision has been made, everyone needs to get on board behind the decision. People who lose the debate and then take losing personally will only serve to poison the team. The last thing you need is someone who is working against the organization's goals just to be able to prove they are right. They may very well have been right, but the point of the team is to act like a team where everyone gives 100 percent toward the team's goals.

The next key to effective teamwork is that everyone not only knows their own job, but they understand how their job fits into the overall picture. I think a characteristic of a successful team is that everyone engages in 360-degree thinking. What I mean by this is that each member not only considers how something impacts them, but also consider how what they are doing will impact the rest of the team. For example, the marketing person needs to consider how their plans impact the sales department or the finance department, and so on.

The point is that while organizations may be divided into departments or divisions, those areas do not and cannot operate in a vacuum. The job of the leader is to create an atmosphere where open communication is expected and followed through with. All groups need to have at least a basic understanding of what the others contribute to the process. This applies to all organizations, both big and small.

SPECIAL NOTE TO PASTORS AND ENTREPRENEURS

Many pastors and entrepreneurs have something in common: they have started an organization from the ground up. Whether you are a pastor who started a church in his living room with five families or the guy who started a business in his garage, there was a time when you were alone. You did it all, from A to Z.

But as the organization grows, at some point a difficult transition needs to take place. In order to reach full effectiveness and be able to scale the business or the church, the pastor or the entrepreneur has to change. The natural thing is for the leader to do what they have always done—everything. However, as the church grows and expands, if the pastor keeps doing everything and never builds a team around him, the church will hit a certain level and it will plateau. It may be at 300 people, it may be at 500, or it may even be at 1,000 people, but it's going to hit a certain level and then stop growing. This will happen because the demands of the church will have begun to exceed the capacity of the pastor.

Once the church hits that level, it will not grow above that pastor's capacity until he builds a team around him and empowers and allows them to free him up. If you've read my book *The Leadership Gap*, you will know the one thing I love to talk about is that the reason for having a staff in the first place is to free up the pastor to do what he does best, that is to be the pastor. That is what God wants from that man, and it's what the church needs to be successful and grow—both numerically and spiritually. If the pastor is so busy putting gas in the bus and cleaning the carpets, he is not busy doing what God has told him to do!

This means a couple of things have to happen: One is that the pastor has to be willing to build the team, let go of them, and allow them to do what God has called them to do. It doesn't do you any good to build the team and then still have a situation where all roads lead to the pastor. If you're going to have a team, you've got to empower them and then, from the standpoint of the team, you've got to be ready to step up and give leadership and direction. You have to understand your calling because, just as that man or woman was called to preach and to lead your congregation, I believe the thing that we really need are people who are called to provide support to the church. We need people who don't want to preach. We need people who want to be on the team. This means that I can impact as many people as Bishop Jakes impacts because I allow him to go and do it.

If it weren't for the team around Bishop Jakes, conferences wouldn't happen. He cannot, as great as he is and as anointed as he is, do it all by himself. It takes a team, and you need to have that team in your church allowing you to do what you do best. And if you don't have them, you need to find those people; because they exist in your congregations. They want to serve; they want to come there and give their very best to the Lord; and they know they can do it. They just need a place to do it. And they need a pastor who will allow them to do it. So you need to find that team, motivate them, and train them. But over time you will need to let go of them, and that's what's going to allow you to be truly effective as a minister and as a leader.

This is a big issue for ministries because all pastors have two sides to their brain just like everybody else. But when it comes to dealing with staff members and employees, the pastor's side of the pastor's brain wants to save that person, and he's worried about their family and about taking care of his staff. But the business side of his brain, the analytical side, knows he needs to do something about that person. So pastors have an internal battle raging within them, which is one reason why people like me exist in our organization, because I guarantee you if we fire somebody it's not Bishop Jakes doing it, it's me doing it because I don't have those pastoral struggles in my brain.

With regard to employees, however, one of the things we need to do is give honest feedback on a consistent basis. Because church people are so nice, we tend to not give honest feedback. So when you let somebody go, it should never be a surprise to that person. It should almost be a relief because if somebody is not performing at their best

in their current position, it's your job as a leader to convey to them the lack of performance and what it is they're
doing right and what it is they're doing wrong, helping
make them better. Our job as leaders is to try to make our
employees better, but sometimes we can't do that. Sometimes we need to realign the person if their skill set doesn't
meet their current job, but maybe they could do something
else within the organization; but sometimes you just have
to cut things off and let them go.

To me personally, as an employer and as a leader, the
really important things really have to do with attitude and
loyalty. If you've got those, I could teach you how to do a lot
of different things, but I can't teach you attitude and loyalty. So if you don't have those attributes then I'm going to
be very quick to let you go. But if you have attitude and loyalty, the proper attitude, a positive attitude, then I'm going
to do a lot of things to try to rehabilitate you to keep you
because I can't teach those things to someone else.

So it really comes down to just needing honesty in the
feedback we give to those around us. People need to know
how they're doing. They need to know where they stand.
But when everyone is in the right place within the organization, then we'll all be successful and fulfill the calling
God has placed on us. In order for the teamwork to be
successful, we, as leaders, need to facilitate it in a deep and
meaningful way.

Chapter 10

RECOGNIZE AND ACKNOWLEDGE WHAT YOU DON'T KNOW

In my business career, some of my most frustrating experiences have involved dealing with people in positions of leadership who don't know (or will not admit that they don't know) what they don't know. I am sure if you think about it, you will soon recall that person who made any situation worse because of their need to "appear" in control and having all the answers. They do much more harm than good.

This is a particular problem among leaders because, by definition, leaders are confident people who like to appear strong. In one of those interesting twists of life, it is those leaders who are humble enough to admit what they don't know who become the strongest and the greatest. How does admitting you don't know something make you a strong leader? Easy: if you can admit you don't know or understand something, you will look to others who know the specific answers you're seeking. As a result, the leader gains knowledge and understanding that they can use to strengthen their position. On the other hand, the leader who doesn't reach out for help will remain in the dark.

Based on my experience, it seems that there are three primary reasons why leaders don't admit what they don't know. And none of the reasons have any merit whatsoever. The first reason people don't seek help is to "save money." I have been guilty of this on more than one occasion when it comes to home repairs. I will say, "Sure I can fix that, I don't need to call the plumber." You can probably guess what happens. Sure enough, I start the project, get into the middle of it, figure out that I have no clue what I am doing, and call the plumber after all. The result is that the cost is more than it would have been had I started with a professional to begin with. In other words, I wasted time and money.

At one point while I was writing this book, my wife, Julaina, was in the hospital. She had emergency surgery to have an infection removed from her leg (she's fine now). As smart as I might think I am, the last thing I could imagine doing in that situation would have been to try to save the doctor's fee and take care of her myself. However, that's exactly what so many leaders do today. In an effort to prove how smart they are and to save a little money, they are killing their organizations.

The world today is extremely complicated and good leaders need to recognize when they need help navigating the waters. By effectively managing and relying on experts (if required) and the rest of the organization's team (if the knowledge and capacity exists on the team), leaders can both broaden their own knowledge and understanding but also get quicker and better answers for difficult situations.

A more problematic situation occurs when the leader will not admit what he doesn't know because of his or her own ego. While the idea of "fake it until you make it" may work in some scenarios, it can be extremely detrimental to the development of an organization.

In my experience working with Bishop Jakes, I saw this problem repeatedly. As I have described, we do business in a lot of varied fields, from books to film to the Internet. However, regardless of the field, the one thing that we know is our audience and how to reach that audience. In fact, a big reason to do business with TDJ Enterprises is that we have access to a distinct audience. A publisher, for example, will want to publish a book with T. D. Jakes because he knows what his audience wants and knows how to reach that audience in order to sell books. So given the foregoing, it never ceases to amaze me that business people will then promptly ignore the very person they are in business with on the topic that is the real reason for the deal to begin with.

It is incredibly frustrating to see a good project, whether it is a book, a music project, a film, or a play, underperform because someone didn't know what they didn't know and insisted on doing it their own way. In my view, the uncommon leader will recognize what he doesn't know and let his partner (who does know that area) do what they do best. The greatest results always come when each side of the business relationship focuses on doing what they do best.

Our most successful film to date, *Jumping the Broom*, is a great example. On this film we partnered with Stage 6 Films (part of Sony Pictures) and Our Stories Films (Tracey Edmunds and Glendon Palmer). This collaboration was a great example of each partner playing to his or her strengths and working well together. Particularly on the marketing and promotion of the film, everyone recognized what they did and did not know. The marketing execs at Sony focused on marketing the film the way they know how to market. In turn, they empowered us to market the film to our audience the way we saw fit. The end result was a great opening weekend and a successful film. The film's success was because everyone focused on what they knew and what they did well.

Within your own organization, the same dynamic comes into play. If the leader is hesitant to get needed help and tries to act as if he knows what he doesn't know, a couple of things will happen. First, the leader's staff will become disillusioned. Nothing is more disheartening than to watch someone who doesn't know what they are doing make mistakes while at the same time rejecting help that could rectify the situation.

In addition, the people the organization does business with will begin to look elsewhere. Why? It is often a frustrating experience to negotiate with and reason with someone who comes from a place of ignorance. I call it negotiating with people who negotiate for the sake of negotiating. They don't have a basis in reality for their positions, so they just negotiate for the sake of it. For example, if someone doesn't know what is a typical business practice in a certain area or what something is worth, then that party is negotiating in the dark. They may not even realize that they are getting a reasonable deal and are being treated well, but they make it hostile for the sake of being a "tough negotiator." The bottom line is that the world works better when you focus on what you know and get expert help when you don't know.

Special Note for the Church

That is what we're doing in our churches as well. There are some things that are outside of the scope of the expertise of the pastor and his staff, but because we're afraid to spend a little bit of money right now, we're killing our church. There are many who have incredible real estate problems right now, but we don't want to spend a little bit of money to get the right guy or the right company who can fix it. Or we don't want to spend a few thousand dollars extra on the right accountant who's going to make our books correct and who's going to be the one who actually tells us that Deacon Billy has been stealing from the church, but nobody's bothered to find a decent accountant to come in and check the church's books. And we don't know that the reason the church doesn't have any money is because Billy's got the money in his bank account.

These, of course, are silly examples, but they get to the point of sometimes we are making these decisions in the name of trying to save a couple of bucks and it's killing our organizations. There are some things where we need to recognize that we just don't know what we're doing here, and it's okay to go outside the church and to bring in somebody who knows what they're really doing. They can help us solve our problems correctly, efficiently, and promptly, so we can get it done and move on. But there is something within us where we just have to do it by ourselves. *We can take care of the problem without anyone's help,* we think to ourselves. *God's going to take care of us and it's all going to be okay.* But the reality is that sometimes you just have to face up that you're in over your head.

By profession I'm a lawyer. I graduated fourth in my law school class. I did incredibly well and I do a lot of legal stuff for Bishop Jakes, but I also know when to hire somebody else because I don't practice law 100 percent of the time anymore, and because I understand the law is incredibly complex and there are some areas where I do not have expertise. I wanted to make sure I had the right surgeon to operate on my wife. Our general practitioner doctor did not do that. We hired the best surgeon for that job.

Sometimes we need to look beyond the church and find the best person for the job. No matter how good we are, no matter what we think about ourselves, there's always somebody better, smarter, and with a little more expertise in certain areas. We need to learn how to use those people, use those resources wisely, and use them in an effective manner. So know what it is that you don't know and admit what it is you don't know, being humble enough to go get some help, and your churches and your ministries will benefit immensely.

As a general matter I would rather engage somebody who is a person of faith to work with me if I can, but I will also not hesitate to go outside to find the right person for the job. Just because the chairman of Sony Pictures is Jewish does not mean that Bishop Jakes cannot have a great relationship with him, and that we can't be partners and use Sony's money to make movies to convey our message. We also sometimes use different lawyers who otherwise might never come to our church, but they have a particular expertise and can solve a particular problem I'm not equipped to solve.

So it really just depends on what the issue is, but sometimes we need to know what we don't know and we need to find the person who does know the answer.

Chapter 11

PUTTING IT ALL TOGETHER: IT'S NOT ABOUT THE SITUATION, IT'S ABOUT THE RESPONSE

Just as we need leaders who have done the work, have true substance, and know the importance of taking time to build a foundation, we also need leaders who know that God is in control of them and their organizations. Because true leaders have done the work and know that God is in control, uncommon leaders recognize that they are not controlled by their circumstances. Quite the opposite: leaders know that it is their response to the situation that matters most. As the Kenny Rogers song says, every hand's a winner and every hand's a loser; what matters is how you play the hand that God deals you. No matter what your hand or situation, somebody could take that same hand and lose with it and someone else could win with it. It's all about the response.

It is inevitable in life and business that struggles will happen. People will do things to offend you. You will be cheated. Things will, at times, not go your way. When something isn't going the way you want, think about what you can learn or how you can benefit from the situation.

Part of God's divine plan is that he has made each of us as unique individuals. There is no other person on earth who has your combination of education and life experience—the good, the bad, or otherwise. Everything that went into your life has gone into making you the person you are today. God has given each of us the gift of a unique place from which to respond to a unique crisis. And so don't, as leaders, undervalue yourself. God gave you those experiences for a reason, to prepare you for something. I don't know what that something is or when it's coming, but you're being prepared for something. And as a leader, you need to focus on the fact that you are being given a crisis to respond to. You can choose to be negative; you can choose to complain about the circumstances; and you can choose to talk about how it's not your fault and finger point and do everything else; but the fact is that none of that is going to do anything about your problem except make it worse.

Leaders respond to the situations, they assess the situation. What is the problem that we have? What are the resources we have to deal with that problem? How are we going to best deploy our resources to fix the problem? That's how true leaders respond. God gave you tools, and you need to use those tools to work the problem, using the creativeness and the uniqueness you have for your advantage. You will have a viewpoint on your problem that nobody else is going to have. That's why you're the one facing that particular problem, and not someone else.

We can all think back to the disaster and the tragedy of 9/11. Aside from politics and aside from whether you were a fan or not a fan, it would be difficult to argue that Mayor Giuliani of New York did not stand up as an exceptional leader in a time of crisis. You might agree or disagree with his politics; but in that moment of crisis he responded in a tremendous way, exercising leadership and courage in the midst of loss and destruction. He clearly had the capacity to respond to that time of crisis.

One of my mentors, Dalton Lott, has a success story that illustrates several points that I have been trying to make. Dalton built a successful sales business as a young man. Unfortunately, his big account went bankrupt and his business partner cheated him. The bottom line is that he went broke and had to start over.

Despite his dire circumstances, Dalton did not let this dictate his result. On the contrary, he had his big idea that he knew would work. So while his wife supported the family on her teacher's salary, he went to work in a small office and started rebuilding his dream. While he was getting started, he was offered a great job. But Dalton knew that his plan would work and so turned the job down. He knew he was on the right course. He did the hard work and kept focused. Today, his business is ten times bigger than it ever was before.

One interesting side note to this story is how Dalton feels about the partner who cheated him. You would expect that he would have feelings of hatred and ill will toward his partner. But the truth is that Dalton has forgiven the man and moved on. He explains that had that man not done what he did, he wouldn't have made the changes he made to his business. He realizes now that he never would have achieved the level of success that he now enjoys had he not had that experience.

We all need to understand that by giving us a situation to deal with, God is giving us an opportunity to learn, grow, and become better. It is all about becoming who God intends us to be. What we have to realize is that we have to do our part. God will give us what we need, but we have to respond in an appropriate way. There is so much wisdom in the simple statement, "When life gives you lemons, make lemonade."

It's All About Making An Impact

I've been very privileged in my life that I've gotten to do a lot of different things, and one of those things is producing five movies now. *Sparkle* is coming out. And *Jumping the Broom* came out not too long ago; and it's a bunch of fun when you go to the premier and actually see the movie. But what you don't see are the two years that went into getting it ready for that moment.

In the film business we call it the development process. It's the longest and the hardest part of the filmmaking process and it all happens before a camera ever rolls and before an actor is ever hired. It is when we're taking that story, shaping it, putting it together, and making sure we're conveying the right message; and then we've got to make sure we hired the right team to capture that story and that we hired the right cast to portray those characters. It's all about building a foundation for that movie to ultimately rest upon. Without all that work up front, the movie would be a disaster.

The question is, Are you ready to do the work to get there? Are we ready to be leaders for modern ministry? Are we ready to take these tools that we've talked about and actually accomplish something? Because it isn't about the top line; it's about the bottom line. The question is when you stop reading this book and you go back to your church, how effective are you being? Are you really impacting lives? That's what it all comes down to at the end of the day. That's the reason we put on events, that's the reason we write the books, and that's the reason we do everything else.

Leadership is all about enabling us to impact lives because it's all in vain if we can't do that and do it effectively. That's my challenge for you at the end of this book. Just remember, if you follow this, the mission is not impossible. You can do this, and we can take the church to heights it has never been to before.

About Curtis Wallace

Mr. Wallace utilizes his unique combination of business and legal experience along with his in-depth knowledge of the faith-based/nonprofit world to guide clients who are navigating the intersection of faith and business. His expertise includes organizational structure, ventures between nonprofit and for-profit entities, entertainment, publishing, real estate matters, financing, and crisis management.

Mr. Wallace is a lawyer and currently serves as the Chief Operating Officer/General Counsel of TDJ Enterprises, LLP. In these capacities, Mr. Wallace works to bring the worlds of faith and business together for the mutual benefit of both.

During his tenure, Mr. Wallace has developed and overseen partnerships with entities including:

- Film production venture with Sony Pictures Entertainment
- Publishing joint venture with Simon and Schuster (Atria Imprint)
- Television and film joint venture with Codeblack Entertainment
- Nationally syndicated radio program with Radio One/Syndication One

Mr. Wallace has served as the producer or executive in charge (on behalf of TDJE/New Dimensions Entertainment) of the following projects:

- The live stage productions *Woman Thou Art Loosed, Behind Closed Doors,* and *Cover Girls*
- The feature films *Woman Thou Art Loosed* (starring Kimberly Elise, released in 2004 by Magnolia Films, and winner of Best American Film at the 2004 Santa Barbara International Film Festival), *Not Easily Broken* (starring Morris Chest-

nut and Taraji P. Henson, released in 2009 by Sony/Tristar), *Jumping the Broom* (starring Angela Bassett and Loretta Devine, released in 2011 by Sony Pictures) *Woman Thou Art Loosed: On the Seventh Day* (starring Blair Underwood and Pam Grier, released in 2012), and most recently, *Sparkle* (starring Jordin Sparks and Whitney Houston, released in 2012 by Sony Pictures).

- "Maximize the Moment" infomercial with Time Life Video
- The creation and touring of the *God's Leading Ladies* conference series
- Multiple music projects released under the Dexterity Sounds label, currently in partnership with Universal Music

Mr. Wallace also works closely with The Potter's House of Dallas, Inc. (founded by Bishop T. D. Jakes) on business, transactional, and IRS compliance matters. Mr. Wallace is also a frequent advisor to nonprofit organizations, as well as a speaker on business, nonprofit, and leadership issues. He has pioneered the Ascension Advisory Group, serving as President and CEO. Ascension is comprised of a team of executives dedicated to working with churches, ministries, pastors, entertainers and businesses seeking success at the intersection of faith and business.

In addition to the foregoing, Mr. Wallace serves on the board of directors of BN Media Holdings, which owns both Affinity 4, an affinity marketing company that has helped nonprofits raise over $76 million to date, and beliefnet.com, the largest website in the spirituality category.

From a community standpoint, Mr. Wallace has previously served on the board of directors of the Parkland Foundation as well as Wycliffe Resources, Inc. Mr. Wallace continues to serve on the Dallas County Blue Ribbon Commission for Parkland Hospital, a group responsible for leading the effort to construct a new $1.2 billion public hospital for the citizens of Dallas.

Prior to joining TDJ Enterprises, Mr. Wallace practiced law, first with Weil, Gotshal & Manges, and later with the firm of Brewer, Brewer, Anthony & Middlebrook, where he headed the firm's transactional practice group. In his legal practice, Mr. Wallace represented individuals, businesses, banks, investment groups, and nonprofit organizations in a diverse array of corporate and real estate transactions ranging from mergers and acquisitions to financing to real estate leases, purchases, and sales.

Mr. Wallace lives in Keller, Texas, with his wife, Julaina, and three sons, Jackson, Harrison, and Carter, and his daughter Caroline.

For more information on how you can take your church or ministry to the next level of excellence, please visit the Ascension Advisory Group online at:

www.ascensionadvisorygroup.com

WANT TO TAKE YOUR LEADERSHIP TO
THE NEXT LEVEL OF EXCELLENCE?

Get the Elevating Excellence curriculum today!
www.elevatingexcellence.org

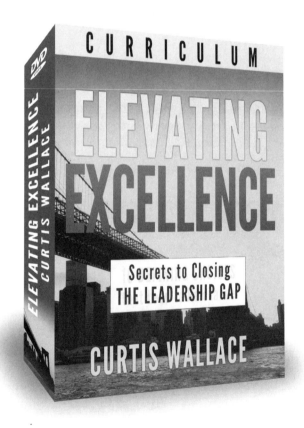